BUILDING CHILDREN'S WOODEN TOYS

Created and designed by the editorial staff of ORTHO BOOKS

Project Editor
Barbara Ferguson Stremple

Project Designer and Writer
Edward A. Baldwin

Technical Writer
Verner W. Clapp

Photographer
Kit Morris

Photographic Stylist
Sara Slavin

Illustrator
Ron Hildebrand

Ortho Books

Publisher
Edward A. Evans

Editorial Director
Christine Jordan

Production Director
Ernie S. Tasaki

Managing Editors
Michael D. Smith
Sally W. Smith

System Manager
Linda M. Bouchard

National Sales Manager
J. D. Gillis

National Accounts Manager—
 Book Trade
Paul D. Wiedemann

Marketing Specialist
Dennis M. Castle

Distribution Specialist
Barbara F. Steadham

Operations Assistant
Georgiann Wright

Administrative Assistant
Francine Lorentz-Olson

Senior Technical Analyst
J. A. Crozier, Jr., Ph.D.

Address all inquiries to:
Ortho Books
Chevron Chemical Company
Consumer Products Division
Box 5047
San Ramon, CA 94583

ISBN 0-89721-214-2
Library of Congress Catalog Card
Number 89-085928

Chevron Chemical Company
6001 Bollinger Canyon Road, San Ramon, CA 94583

Acknowledgments

Copy Chief
Melinda Levine

Editorial Coordinator
Cass Dempsey

Copyeditor
Rebecca Pepper

Proofreader
Deborah Bruner

Indexer
Shirley J. Manley

Editorial Assistants
Nancy McCune
John Parr

Composition by
Laurie A. Steele

Layout & production by
Studio 165

Illustration Assistants
Joanne Brannigan
Anne Marie Hamill
Angela Hildebrand
David Hildebrand
Frank Hildebrand
Jason Hildebrand
Jim Todd

*Projects and photo
backgrounds painted by*
Surface Studios
San Francisco, Calif.

Photography Assistant
Doug Workmaster

Separations by
Color Tech Corporation

Lithographed in the USA by
Webcrafters, Inc.

Front cover
Clockwise from top: Pony Rocker (page 74), Ring Toss Game (page 88), Balls in a Cage (page 24), Noah's Ark (page 34), and center, Circus Train (page 46).

Page 1: Handmade wooden toys make wonderful gifts. Instructions for this biplane are on page 69.

Page 3: Little Red Wagon, page 50

Back cover
Top left: Rocking Dinosaur, page 78

Top right: Ball-Wheel Racer, page 30

Bottom left: Bobbing Turtle, page 41

Bottom right: Doll Cradle, page 90

BUILDING CHILDREN'S WOODEN TOYS

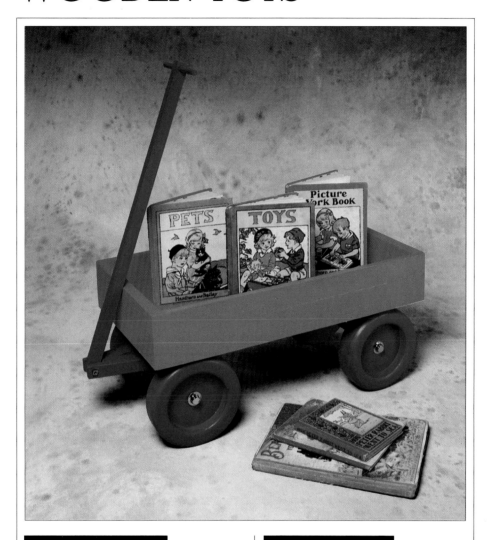

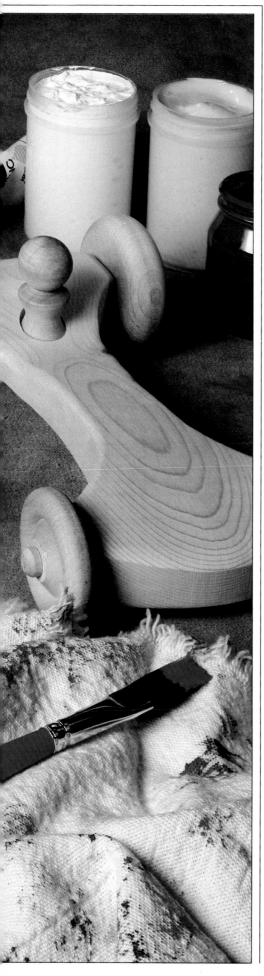

TIPS, TOOLS, AND TECHNIQUES

Every toymaker has his or her own method of making toys. Ever since Geppetto made Pinocchio, people have been coming up with designs that fascinate, entertain, teach, and occupy young minds, hands, and feet. Making wooden toys is a pleasant and relaxing hobby that can bring many hours of enjoyment to both you and the recipients of your labors. The toys you make must, however, be safe for a young child to use. The key is to use the right wood, fasteners, adhesives, hardware, and finishes, and to put it all together correctly.

With the proper tools, even the beginning woodworker can construct all of the toys in this book. Most can be made with basic hand tools, but power tools, and the techniques made possible by their use, further simplify the construction of these projects. The section that follows lists the power tools most useful for making toys.

Also included in this chapter is a discussion of the best woods to use for the toys in this book and how the different woods are sized. General tips on how to glue, finish, sand, dowel, and join wood materials are also given here; refer to them as you put together a project. The hints for making toys safe for children will give you insight into what to watch for and how to avoid making an unsafe toy. A list of sources that carry different toy-building supplies, including specialty woods and small wood parts such as wheels, balls, dowels, and axle pegs, can be found at the end of this chapter.

Finishing the toys is one of the most enjoyable steps in building them. There are many options: Clear varnish works well on attractive woods, spray paint is easy and quick to apply, and hand-painting with a brush is very satisfying and allows you to be more creative.

WOODWORKING BASICS

Before starting on a project, take a few minutes to read through the information in this chapter. The tips provided here on selecting materials, using tools, and simplifying tasks will save you time and ensure that the projects are well made.

Power Tools

Toymaking does not require a lot of tools if you are going to make something only once in a blue moon. However, if you will be working with wood on a regular basis, power tools are the best answer. Some applications are ideal for hand tools, others are best for hand-held power tools, and some require the use of stationary power tools.

Hand-held power tools are widely available at almost all discount stores, department stores, and hardware stores across the country. You can buy drills, portable drill press stands, sanders, and jigsaws at a cost of only $15 to $40. Today, the basic home workshop toolbox should have, at a minimum, a ⅜-inch electric hand-held drill, a vibrating-pad sander, and a jigsaw or saber saw if any serious woodworking is contemplated. If your projects include carpentry, you should also have a hand-held power circular saw. Other desirable portable power tools include a belt sander and a router.

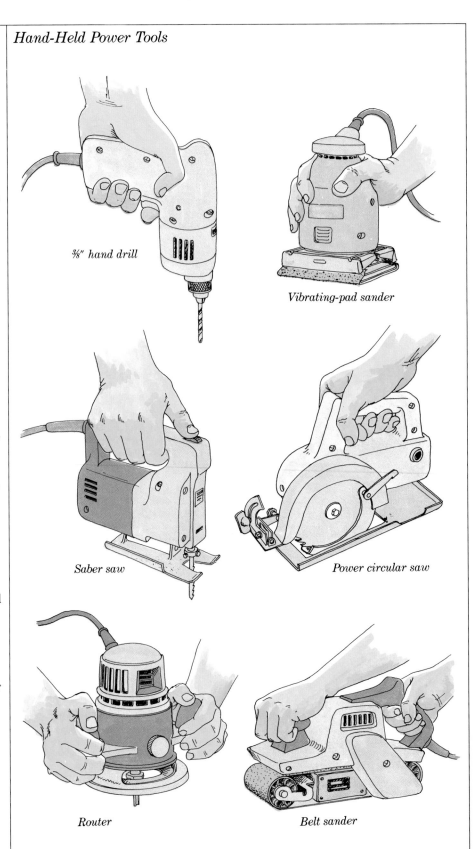

Hand-Held Power Tools

⅜" hand drill

Vibrating-pad sander

Saber saw

Power circular saw

Router

Belt sander

Benchtop Stationary Tools

Table saw

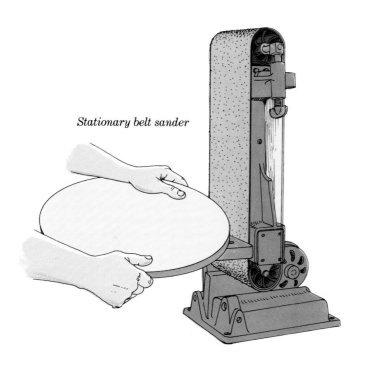

Stationary belt sander

In addition to these tools, many smaller benchtop stationary tools, such as table saws, scroll saws, band saws, and drill presses, are quite handy and cost around $100 to $200. The table saw is the tool to purchase first on this list. It is invaluable for many of the saw cuts made for these toys and many other home workshop projects. The stationary belt sander (or portable belt sander with a stand) is another very useful tool, especially for projects in this book.

Even if you don't own all of the required power tools, they often are available from a friend, a school woodworking shop, or a public hobby center. For example, most military bases have hobby woodworking shops, as do many retirement centers.

All of these power tools make the construction of even simple projects, such as many of these wooden toys, immeasurably easier. In most cases, the parts fit better, and the results are more satisfactory and of higher quality.

Tools and Techniques

The great advantage to having many tools available to you is that they permit you to use many timesaving techniques. The sections that follow give various methods for making the required cuts in these projects and for creating some of your own materials, as well as ways to save time. You will also find information on gluing, sanding, and finishing your projects, as well as tips on gluing dowels and using fastening hardware.

Straight Cuts

The tools of choice for straight, square, and angled cuts are the table saw or radial arm saw with good, smooth-cut carbide or steel cabinet blades. The table saw is best and safest for making rip cuts or cutting thin, small pieces. You can also use a band saw, if it is equipped with a fence and miter gauge, although the cut is not as smooth or straight as the cut from a circular blade.

A word of warning is appropriate here: Sawing thin, narrow, and small pieces can be dangerous with any of these saws. Fingers get very close to the moving blade, and pieces can jam between the saw and fence and be thrown. Saw from the outside of a larger piece, if possible. Get help when cutting out these pieces if you are not thoroughly familiar with the saw or the technique.

If stationary power tools are not available, a handsaw can certainly be used for most of the required straight cuts. A jigsaw or saber saw will do the job as well, but they make it difficult to maintain a straight line, and some follow-up rasping or sanding will be necessary. A hand-held power circular saw will also work for many of the straight cuts.

Curved Cuts

The tool of choice for all of the curved cuts is also a stationary power saw, in this case a band saw or scroll saw. Use a narrow blade with fine teeth for the small-radius cuts. The band saw is limited to outside cuts only. The bench scroll saw cuts more slowly and is limited by the stock thickness, but it is better for the more intricate cuts and the inside cuts.

The hand-held power jigsaw or saber saw is another excellent tool for making curved cuts in stock up to 1½ inches thick. One advantage of this type of saw is its ability to make a plunge cut to get the saw blade into enclosed or inside circles or shapes. If power equipment is not available, a hand coping saw works well. Both the coping saw and the scroll saw have removable blades. You can gain access to an inside cut by predrilling a saw-blade entrance hole, inserting the blade through the hole, and reattaching the blade to the saw.

The throat depth of the frame of the coping saw, the scroll saw, and the band saw limits the reach of these inside cuts. However, this should not be a problem with the smaller work found in most of these wooden toy projects.

Stationary Scroll Saw or Jigsaw

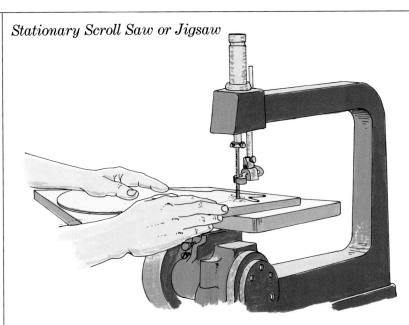

Holes

The smaller holes (½ inch or less) can easily be drilled with a hand-held electric drill or drill press, using twist drill bits. Brad-pointed bits, if available, are best for drilling wood. They center quickly and tend not to skate sideways when starting the hole. Use higher speeds when drilling the smaller holes, and whenever possible use a backup wood scrap to prevent the drill from tearing the grain when it exits the piece.

Some of the toy projects call for larger holes (¾ inch to 3 inches in diameter). These large holes present different problems and require different cutting tools. A spur or Forstner bit or a hole saw (some come in sets) work well. An adjustable circle cutter (also called a fly cutter) will also do the job. Caution: Use the circle cutter only in a drill press. It is dangerous to use in a hand-held drill. Always use a backup piece to keep the grain from tearing when the tool emerges.

If a bit, circle cutter, or hole saw is not available in the correct diameter, you can saw the hole, guiding it by hand. A jigsaw is excellent for this when used in conjunction with a plunge cut. Use a stiffer, wider blade to make the plunge, and then change to a narrow blade to cut the hole. The

coping saw and scroll saw are excellent tools for making narrow-radius or delicate inside cuts. With these two tools, you must first bore a saw-blade entrance hole.

Cutting Thin Stock

Some of the toy projects call for thin (less than ¾ inch) solid wood stock, which may be difficult to find on the shelf at a lumberyard. In such cases, you may need to reduce 1-inch lumber (¾ inch thick) to the necessary thickness. You have several options:
• Substitute plywood, hardboard, or particleboard. This may not be a good alternative because of the rough, end-grain edge of plywood or for strength reasons.
• See if your lumberyard has a planer or resaw and can machine your stock to the required thickness.
• Take your purchased ¾-inch material to a neighborhood cabinet shop. Most have planers and resawing equipment and are willing to do custom work.
• Do the job yourself, using your own or a friend's woodworking equipment. You can obtain the needed thickness either by planing a thicker piece down to the required thickness or by resawing.

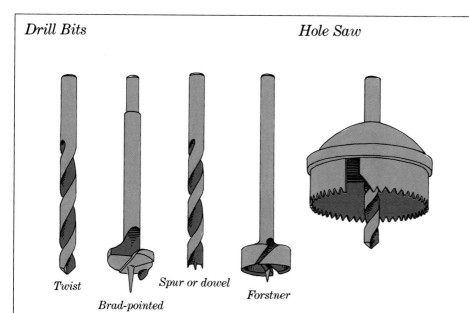

Drill Bits

Hole Saw

Twist

Brad-pointed

Spur or dowel

Forstner

If you have access to a planer, you are fortunate. If the stock you need is greater than ⅜ inch thick, make several passes, surfacing the lumber down to the final thickness. If you need material that is less than ⅜ inch thick, it is most economical to first resaw the 1-inch stock, ripping it on edge in half, and then plane to the final thickness.

If a planer is not available, you can get the desired thickness by sawing. A band saw with a fence and wide blade is the preferred (and safest) tool to do this job. It will leave a rough-sawn face that must be passed over a jointer or smoothed by sanding.

You can also use a table saw, but the depth of cut is limited. (The piece can be flipped over, however, in effect doubling the cut depth.) Use the smoothest-cut rip or combination blade you have. Of course, with either a band saw or a table saw, first rip the pieces to the required width to keep the depth of the cut to a minimum when resawing.

If you do resaw lumber on either a band or table saw, take special caution—a lot of blade is exposed. The use of a push stick is mandatory. Hold-downs should also be used. Beware of the thin pieces becoming caught between the saw and fence and being thrown.

Duplicate Sawing or Drilling

A number of the wooden toy designs in this book call for two or more pieces to be cut or drilled to the same pattern. The patterns usually call for curved saw cuts. Frequently, the required pieces can be stacked and either gang-cut on the band saw, the scroll saw, or the jigsaw, or gang-drilled. The edges can also be gang-sanded. This assures perfectly matched pieces and saves work. The problem is how to hold the pieces firmly together while sawing and then separate them easily with a minimum of damage to the wood surface. There are several ways to do this:
• Hold the pieces together with clamps. A common problem with this method is that the clamps get in the way when you saw or drill.
• Tack the pieces together with fine wire brads. After you have sawed out the pattern, pull the pieces apart, remove the brads, and fill the holes with wood filler. You can also position the brad holes in parts of the pieces that will not be seen or that will later be cut out.
• Use double-stick carpet tape. Most hardware or carpet stores have this.
• Use several very small drops of hot-melt adhesive (from a glue gun). The pieces should pry apart easily with a

minimum of damage to the surfaces after sawing. Scrape or sand off any residual glue.
• Place a small amount of woodworking glue on the first piece, cover it with a piece of bond paper, and then put some more glue on the paper. Place the second piece on the first, sandwiching the paper between.

However you join the pieces, be careful to orient them so that if any damage to the surface occurs with the temporary joining, it will be to the poorer face. For example, when using AC-grade plywood, match and glue the two C faces together.

Making Your Own Wheels
Many of these toy projects call for wood wheels. The larger wheels, of course, have to be sawn out. Some of the materials lists call for preturned hardwood wheels (and axle pegs), which can be purchased at hobby shops or specialty woodworking stores. These wheels are attractive and well made.

You may not be able to find a ready supply of the turned wheels, however, or you may wish to make your own. Two tools work well for this. One is a hole saw with a center drill bit. The other is a circle cutter. As was mentioned earlier, hole saws frequently come in sets so that you have a choice of diameters. The circle cutters are adjustable. Again, a caution: Use the circle cutter only in a fixed drill press, and watch your hands and fingers.

The center drill bit is usually ¼ inch in diameter. If you need a larger axle hole, you can bore out the center hole with a larger bit. If you need a smaller hole, you can glue a ¼-inch dowel in the existing hole and then drill a smaller axle hole in it. Be sure to use a piece of scrap wood under the work to keep the wood from splitting when the saw or cutter cuts through. Sand the edges of the wheel round.

Axle pegs can be made from a dowel. Cut a short piece of a larger dowel, drill a hole in it the same diameter as the axle dowel, and then glue it to the end of the axle dowel.

Blind Holes and Drill Stops

A number of the projects require blind holes, that is, ones that are drilled a specific depth into the wood but do not pass all the way through. This requires the use of a drill stop.

If you are using a drill press, you can control the hole depth very easily by using the built-on depth stop. All drill presses have them. If you are using a hand-held drill, a number of commercially made stops are available that clamp into position on the drill bit. Another technique is to drill a hole with the selected drill bit through a small piece of dowel or wood, cut to the proper length. Slide it onto the drill bit and then adjust the final depth by sliding the bit in or out in the drill chuck.

Clamps and Vises

Almost all the projects in this book require some clamping. Four- or five-inch C-clamps should do the job. If available, several small bar clamps are also useful. There are occasions when several strong rubber bands work well to hold small pieces together for gluing.

Clamps can leave ugly mars, especially in softwoods such as pine. Pads, made from scraps of thin wood or other smooth material, should be used to prevent this. Use waxed paper between the work and the pads to prevent sticking if the wood has any glue on it.

The jaws of woodworking vises are smooth to prevent damage to the work. However, many home workshops have only a metal vise available. In this case, take the same precautions used with clamps: Place pads between the vise jaws and the work to prevent marring.

Gluing

Since most of these toy projects are for indoor use, waterproof glue is not needed. The common white and yellow woodworking glues (polyvinyl and aliphatic resin glues) are the best for most of these toy projects. If the toy is going to be exposed to the elements, urea formaldehyde resin glue (it comes in powder form and is mixed with water) is better but still not completely waterproof. The best waterproof glue, resorcinol resin glue, consists of a liquid resin and catalyst powder, which must be mixed together. It is strong and waterproof but it is not handy to use, has a short shelf life, and leaves a dark purple stain wherever it is applied.

Epoxy glue is fine for small pieces. Silicone sealer/glue is waterproof but not very strong. It works fairly well when used in conjunction with nails and is a good sealer. Model airplane cement is good for small pieces where a short drying time is desirable and strength is not very important. Hot-melt adhesive (used in conjunction with a glue gun) is good for some purposes but has the disadvantage of making it difficult to get a tight joint. Check at your favorite hardware store—new glues are always arriving on the market.

Drill stops

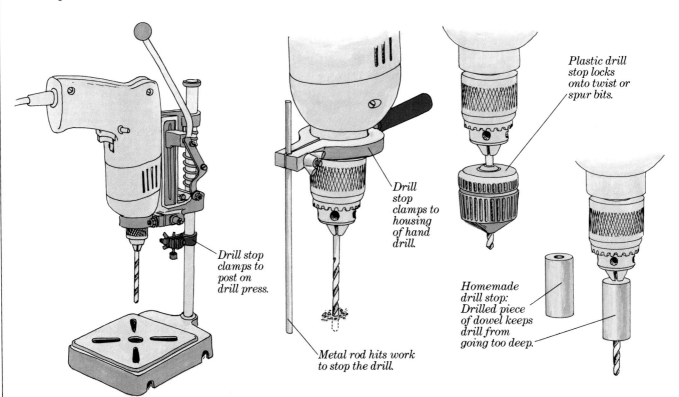

Drill stop clamps to post on drill press.

Drill stop clamps to housing of hand drill.

Metal rod hits work to stop the drill.

Plastic drill stop locks onto twist or spur bits.

Homemade drill stop: Drilled piece of dowel keeps drill from going too deep.

When applying glue, be careful not to use too much. This is especially true if you will be using a clear finish. The glue, even if wiped off, prevents the wood from darkening when finish is applied. If excess woodworking glue does squeeze from the joint, quickly clean it off with a wet rag. When the joint is dry, lightly sand the area next to the joint before applying the finish.

Gluing dowels. Take care when gluing dowels in blind holes. If you use too much glue and the fit is tight, the hydraulic pressure generated when the dowel is driven in can split the parent wood. Make a groove or flatten the side of the dowel to allow excess glue to escape, and use a minimum amount of glue.

Sanding
Since many of these projects have curved sawn surfaces, a rasp or coarse sandpaper (less than 80 grit) is needed to remove the saw marks. Next, all surfaces should be sanded with medium sandpaper (80 to 120

Flat-Headed Wood Screws

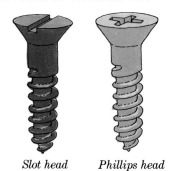

Slot head   Phillips head

Countersinking Screws

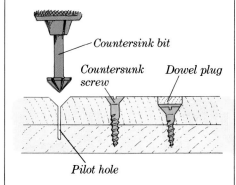

Countersink bit

Countersunk   Dowel plug
screw

Pilot hole

grit) to round the edges and smooth the surfaces. Finally, the projects should be sanded smooth just before finishing with fine (150 to 180 grit) paper. Follow this procedure on all the projects.

Hand-sanding is laborious at best. If you are sanding by hand, sanding blocks are useful. Many types of power sanders are available, from inexpensive vibrating-pad sanders to belt and disk sanders, both portable and stationary. You should have or borrow one of these.

Finishing
Toys, or parts of toys, often end up in children's mouths. Be sure that any finish you use, especially if you choose a colorful paint, is nontoxic. Most state this on the label. Clear finishes, such as varnish or lacquer, are less likely to have potentially toxic pigments in them. A clear finish looks great on an attractive wood. Pressure spray paint and clear finishes are the simplest to use. They are easy to apply, give good results, and are easy to clean up. If you do use the spray cans, be sure to follow the instructions on the cans and use them in a well-ventilated location away from any source of ignition.

Hard wax is a good clear finish for the simpler toys, especially if the wood is a denser hardwood such as maple or birch. Use a prepared wax finish such as a Minwax product or a paste furniture wax. These are reasonably durable and give a soft luster that highlights the wood grain.

Fastening Hardware
The proper screw to use in woodworking is a flat-headed wood screw with a slotted, Phillips, or square recess head for driving. Drill a pilot hole in all cases, and countersink the entrance to the hole so that the screw head is flush. If you really want to get fancy, recess the screw head in a predrilled hole, fill the hole with a wood plug or a dowel, and sand it flush.

If you use nails or brads as fasteners, finishing or headless nails should be used. Countersink the head with

a nail set and then fill the holes with wood filler. If the filler shrinks while drying, apply a bit more. Sand the filler flush after it has dried.

Wood Materials
There are many good species of wood for these projects and a few that are not so good. Most of the common 2 by 4 and 2 by 6 construction woods found in the neighborhood lumberyard, such as Douglas fir, southern yellow pine, larch, and hemlock, are not suitable. They are coarse, grainy, and split easily, and they are frequently sold green and have a high moisture content. To build these toys, you need a dry, even-textured, split-resistant wood.

Softwoods (Conifers)
Although they mar easily, softwoods are light and easy to cut, shape, and sand. The best softwoods to use are the soft pines such as white pine, ponderosa (western yellow) pine, and sugar pine. Spruce is also a good choice. Cedar, redwood, and true (white or balsam) fir are a bit coarser and split easily, but they can certainly be used.

Hardwoods (Broadleaf or Deciduous)
Hardwoods are more even textured and durable than softwoods. They also look great when given a natural finish, but the harder species are more difficult to work with. Hard maple, cherry, birch, and oak are beautiful woods (hard maple and birch are the traditional choices for wooden toys), but they are expensive, hard to find, and difficult to saw, shape, drill, and sand. Alder, poplar, soft maple, and mahogany are softer and easier to work with. Usually at least one lumberyard or woodworking store in a town stocks some of the more common hardwoods.

No matter what type of wood you choose, be sure it is dry; otherwise the glue will fail, the wood will shrink and warp, and the finish may end up with blemishes.

Plywood

If you use plywood in a wooden toy project, birch or other hardwood plywood is best. The more common construction-grade plywood made of Douglas fir or southern pine is coarse, splits easily, and frequently has internal voids. (An exception might be AC-grade Douglas fir or AA-sanded plywood.) Strandboard or wafer construction board is usually not a good choice. Many medium-density or high-density particleboards or hardboards are satisfactory but are not strong enough for some uses. All plywood and boards are usually dry.

Lumber Sizes

The various types of wood available are measured and sized differently. Surfaced dimension (construction) and select or common-grade pine lumber is sold as 1 by 4, 2 by 4, 2 by 6, and so on, but the wood is not really that size. It measures anywhere from ¼ inch to ⅝ inch smaller. For instance, a 1 by 4 is really ¾ inch by 3½ inches, a 1 by 12 is ¾ inch by 11¼ inches, and a 2 by 6 is 1½ inches by 5½ inches when dry. If the wood is green, the actual size is going to be slightly thicker and wider. Actual plywood thicknesses are correct; ¼-inch plywood is ¼ inch thick.

Shop-grade pine and hardwood lumber is sold in thicknesses measured in quarters of an inch. For example, 4/4 is 1 inch thick, 5/4 is 1¼ inches thick, 8/4 is 2 inches thick, and so on. These thicknesses are rough; surfaced lumber is ¼ inch or more thinner. Widths are random, from 3 inches to 15 inches.

The toy projects in this book frequently call for 2 by 4 pine, which is actually 1½ inches thick. Soft pine 2 by 4s are not always a common lumberyard item. As a substitute, you can glue two pieces of 1 by 4 together before cutting the wood to shape. Use protective pads to keep the clamp from marring the wood.

The thinner ¼-inch to ⅝-inch surfaced lumber can also be difficult to find. To make your own see Cutting Thin Stock on page 8.

Stock Lumber Sizes

Surfaced construction softwoods and select- or common-grade pine

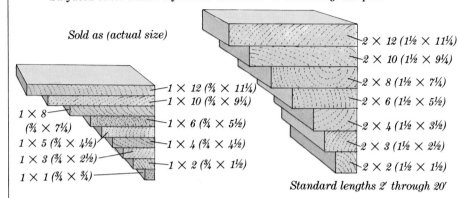

Sold as (actual size)

1 × 12 (¾ × 11¼)
1 × 10 (¾ × 9¼)
1 × 8 (¾ × 7¼)
1 × 6 (¾ × 5½)
1 × 5 (¾ × 4½)
1 × 4 (¾ × 4½)
1 × 3 (¾ × 2½)
1 × 2 (¾ × 1½)
1 × 1 (¾ × ¾)

2 × 12 (1½ × 11¼)
2 × 10 (1½ × 9¼)
2 × 8 (1½ × 7¼)
2 × 6 (1½ × 5½)
2 × 4 (1½ × 3½)
2 × 3 (1½ × 2½)
2 × 2 (1½ × 1½)

Standard lengths 2′ through 20′

Hardwoods and Shop-Grade Pine

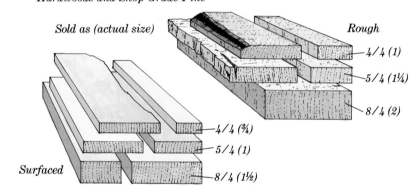

Sold as (actual size)

Rough
4/4 (1)
5/4 (1¼)
8/4 (2)

4/4 (¾)
5/4 (1)
Surfaced
8/4 (1½)

Transferring Shapes From Illustrations

Check the instructions for size of material; check the illustration for size of grid squares.

Draw a grid pattern on your work with squares the size specified on the drawing. Mark where the pattern crosses each grid line, then connect the marks to draw the pattern.

Several projects call for very thin or narrow pieces for edging, railings, and trim. You can saw these out, but again, if you do this on a power saw, be extremely careful. Fingers get very close to moving blades. As an alternative, look through the molding bins at your lumberyard or building-supply store. A number of common molding patterns could be substituted. Hobby shops are also good sources of thin and narrow stock.

Wood Wheels and Balls

Many of the toy projects in this book make use of preturned hardwood wheels, axle pegs, and balls. These are not commonly available at hardware stores or lumberyards. They may be available at hobby shops or specialty woodworking stores. If you cannot find them locally, try the woodworking supply mail-order houses listed under Sources below.

Transferring Shapes From Illustrations

Before cutting out a piece, you need to transfer the shape from the illustration to your work. Frequently, the outline of the piece needs to be enlarged. The time-tested way to do this is to use a grid. Draw the enlarged grid on the work or on a piece of cardboard for a pattern, and transfer the shape, square for square, from the grid on the illustration. The illustrations will tell you what size grid to use.

If the illustration is given at full size, you can trace it and then transfer it to the work, using carbon paper or sewing transfer paper. Another method is to photocopy the illustration, cut it out, and use it as a pattern. Some photocopy machines will also make enlargements. Usually the maximum enlargement is 150 percent, so you may have to make it in two or more steps to reach the desired size.

Making Toys Safe for Children

When you make toys, be certain that they are appropriate for the age of the intended recipient. Never give children under three years old toys that have small parts that can break easily or be swallowed. The Marvelous Gear Machine should not be given to a young child who might stick his or her finger in the gears. Some of the games require skills that only older children have developed, so please keep the age of the child in mind when constructing the toy. Each project introduction gives a suggested age range for the toy.

Check your child's toys periodically to make certain they are in good working order. Check all fittings and joints to be sure that they have not come loose. Check for loose parts or splinters that could harm your child. Make certain that all finishes are nontoxic. Read the labels of all finishing chemicals carefully. Be sure that the wood you use is not a treated variety suitable only for outdoor building projects. Some people are allergic to certain woods. If your young person has an allergy problem, finish and seal the toy thoroughly.

Remove any rough edges on toys by thoroughly sanding them. Make certain that all metal parts are smooth and have no burrs or sharp edges. If you use plywood, check that the edges are properly filled and sealed. Also be sure that all nail and screw heads are recessed and covered with filler or wood plugs.

Do not use ordinary household string or monofilament as a pull cord on pull toys. Use the plastic variety sold at craft stores. You can also use floating fly line used for fly-fishing; get the least expensive brand you can find. Regular string or monofilament can hurt little fingers and entangle arms and legs.

Many of the toys in this book should not be left outdoors. Rain and the elements quickly cause the paint to fade and the parts to become loose—shortening their life span.

Sources

The following mail-order companies supply turned solid hardwood wheels, spoked wheels, axle pegs, solid wood balls, little people, dowels, and some specialty woods. You can write or call for a catalog. Other sources of supplies are usually listed in the back of woodworking magazines.

Bob Morgan's Woodworking Supply
1123 Bardstown Rd.
Louisville, KY 40204
502-456-2545

Cherry Tree Toys, Inc.
Box 369
Belmont, OH 43718
614-484-4363

Craftsman Wood Service
1735 Cortland Ct.
Addison, IL 60101
800-543-9367 (orders)
312-629-3100 (info.)

Trendlines, Inc.
357 Beacham St.
Chelsea, MA 02150
800-343-3248

Woodcraft
41 Atlantic Ave.
Woburn, MA 01888
617-935-6414

Woodworker's Supply of New Mexico
5604 Alameda Place, NE
Albuquerque, NM 87113
800-645-9292

Timbers Woodworking Catalog
Box 850
Carnelian Bay, CA 95711-0850
916-581-4141

Meisel Hardware
Box 70
Mound, MN 55364-0070
800-441-9870

The Woodworker Store
21801 Industrial Blvd.
Rogers, MN 55374-9514
612-428-2899

Constantines
2050 Eastchester Rd.
Bronx, NY 10461
800-223-8087

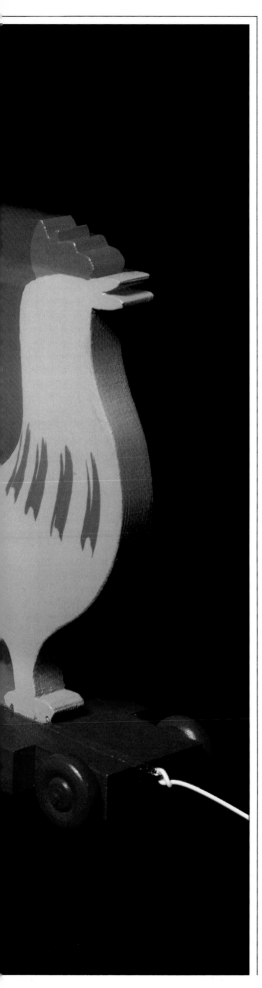

PUSH AND PULL TOYS

I n this chapter are toys for the youngest of the young. For toddlers, the Bouncing Chicken Family, the Babies in a Boat, the Wobbling Goose Family, the Balls in a Cage, and Noah's Ark, complete with several pairs of animals, are all good choices. The Super Racers, the Dumping Pickup Truck, the Farm Tractor, the Circus Train, the Bobbing Turtle, and the Little Red Wagon appeal to both toddlers and preschoolers.

For the most part, these are the simplest projects to build. They can be made with hand tools, although they go together faster if you have access to some basic power tools. Many of these toys can be made in a few hours or over a weekend. All make delightful gifts.

The Bouncing Chicken Family (see page 16) needs only an enthusiastic toddler to tow it around the house. The bounce and wobble are built in.

BOUNCING CHICKEN FAMILY

*T*his family—a mother hen and two chicks—is as much fun to make as it is to watch in action. The wheels are offset on the axles so that the chickens bounce up and down as they are pulled across the floor. This project is geared for the one- to four-year-old age group.

It is best to cut out the curved shapes and details of this project with a hand coping saw or a power scroll saw. If you use a very narrow blade, you can also make most of the cuts with a hand-held power jigsaw or saber saw. Other tools needed include a drill with ⅛-inch, 3/16-inch, 7/32-inch, and ¼-inch drill bits, a narrow chisel, and the standard hand tools. See the comments in Tools and Techniques on page 7.

Building Steps

1. Trace the body outlines of the mother hen and chicks from the illustrations, and transfer them to ¾-inch stock. See Transferring Shapes From Illustrations on page 13. Carefully saw out the shapes with a coping saw, jigsaw, or scroll saw.

What two-year-old could resist pulling this hen and her chicks around? As they roll, the figures bob and sway.

Materials List

Soft pine, spruce, or soft hardwoods such as alder or poplar, ¾ inch thick, work well for this project. A 3-foot piece of 1 by 8 should do the job. Cut the pieces from areas between knots and other defects. They should be clear and reasonably straight grained. See Wood Materials, page 11. In all, you will need one 3-foot length of 3/16-inch dowel and one 6-inch length of ¼-inch dowel.

Lumber

Piece	No. of Pieces	Thickness	Width	Length
Hen body	1	¾"	6"	9"
Chick bodies	2	¾"	5"	5½"
Hen platform	1	¾"	3¼"	5"
Chick platforms	2	¾"	2⅞"	4"
Hen axles	2	3/16" dowel	3"	
Chick axles	4	3/16" dowel	2⅞"	
Pivot rods	3	3/16" dowel	2½"	
Wheel-hole plugs	12	¼" dowel	⅜"	

Hardware and Miscellaneous

Item	Quantity	Size	Description
Wood wheels	8	3/16" × 1"	Turned hardwood wheels
Wood wheels	4	⅜" × 1½"	Turned hardwood wheels
Screw eyes	5	3/16" dia	Bright, plated
Plastic cord	1	60"	
Glue	1 small bottle		Woodworking
Sandpaper	2 sheets	100–150 grit	Medium and fine
Finish	1–2 cans		2 colors, enamel

Hen and Chick Pattern on 1" Squares

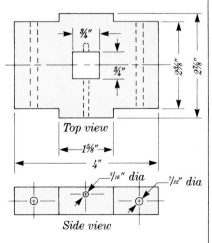

Plug center hole by gluing in a piece of dowel and sanding smooth.

Drill new hole off-center

1" wheels

⁷/₃₂" dia

⁷/₃₂" dia

Hen Platform Pattern

¾"

¾"

2¼"

3¼"

Top view

2"

5"

³/₁₆" dia

⁷/₃₂" dia

Side view

Chick Platform Pattern

¾"

¾"

2⅜"

2⅞"

Top view

1⅝"

4"

³/₁₆" dia

⁷/₃₂" dia

Side view

2. Cut out the hen and chick platforms. Copy the outline from the drawing, including the square center holes, and saw the shapes. Drill a ¼-inch-diameter saw-blade entrace hole in the center of each platform, then saw out the ¾-inch-square block. Use a wood chisel to square the corners of these cutouts. (A mortising chisel or bit works well, if available.)

3. The wheels probably already have a centered axle hole drilled in them. The bounce in the Bouncing Chicken Family comes from off-center axles. You must plug the center holes and drill new offset ones. The existing axle holes are probably ¼ inch in diameter, but check to make sure. Plug the center hole in each wheel with a short piece of ¼-inch dowel (or a dowel that matches the size of the hole), and glue in place. Sand or rasp flush.

4. Drill the new offset axle holes, taking care not to splinter the edges. The new holes will be ³/₁₆ inch in diameter. Offset the holes approximately ⅛ inch from the wheel center. Do not make this offset too great or the wheel won't turn easily.

5. Set the wheels aside. While you still have the ³/₁₆-inch bit in the drill, bore the pivot holes in the 3 platforms. Locate these holes carefully, following the illustrations. Drill them about 2½ inches deep into and through the center of the square cutouts in the centers of the platforms. The holes must be straight and square. Use a drill press if available.

6. Using a ⁷/₃₂-inch bit, drill the axle holes through the 3 platforms, as shown in the illustrations. As with the pivot holes, these must be straight and square. Check the fit of the ³/₁₆-inch dowel stock in these holes. If the dowel does not turn freely, redrill the holes with a ¼-inch bit.

7. Next, drill a ⁷/₃₂-inch hole in the bottom of the hen and chick bodies. Note the exact location in the illustration. These holes must also be straight. Use a ¼-inch drill bit if your previous test showed the ³/₁₆-inch dowels fit too tightly.

Hen and Chick Assembly

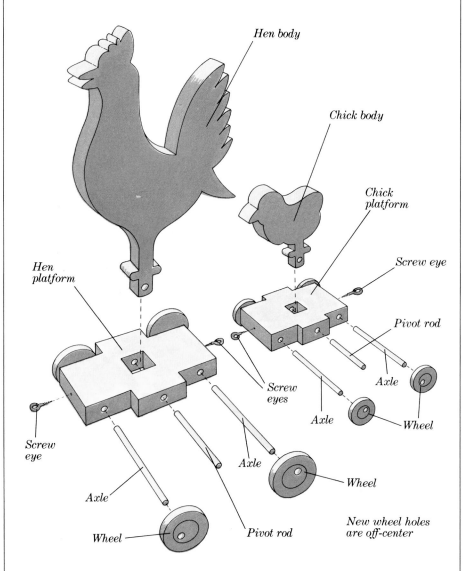

Hen body

Chick body

Chick platform

Screw eye

Hen platform

Axle

Pivot rod

Screw eyes

Axle

Wheel

Screw eye

Axle

Wheel

Axle

Pivot rod

New wheel holes are off-center

Wheel

8. Cut the ³/₁₆-inch dowel to the various lengths for the hen and chick axles and the 3 pivot rods. Lightly sand them with fine-grit sandpaper after cutting to length. Don't overdo this on the ends of the axles—they must fit snugly into the wheel holes.

9. Check the final fit. Assemble the parts, but don't drive the dowels in so deep or tight that they cannot be removed. Sand the dowels a little more where needed for a snug, but not tight, fit.

Make sure the bodies rock freely back and forth on the platforms. If the wheels are aligned with each other on the axles, the bouncing action will be up and down. When the wheels are offset, the motion will also be sideways.

10. Make any final adjustments needed. Begin the final sanding with a rasp to smooth all the sharp or coarse curves, corners, and edges. Then sand, progressing from medium-grit to fine-grit sandpaper, removing saw marks, rounding edges, and smoothing all surfaces. Wipe off all sawdust.

11. It might be best to finish all the parts before final assembly. Spray paint does a good job and saves much fuss and bother. A quick-drying enamel or lacquer works well. Give all the pieces at least 2 coats. Don't paint the dowels.

12. Now begin the final assembly. Attach the bodies to the platform. This time add glue to the last inch or so of the pivot dowels. Insert the axle dowels through the platforms, add a small amount of glue to the ends, and attach the wheels. Align the wheels for the desired offset before the glue sets. Take care to insert or drive the dowels flush with the sides of the wheels and platforms. Wipe off any excess glue at this time with a damp rag or sponge.

13. When everything is dry, you will probably want to touch up the bare dowel ends with matching paint. Spray them directly or spray them, if you prefer, onto a piece of paper and use a small paintbrush to touch up the dowel ends. You may also elect to paint some trim with contrasting paint on the hen and chick bodies, outlining their eyes, feathers, and wings.

14. Attach the screw eyes. (Note their locations on the illustrations.) Using the plastic cord, tie the mother hen and the 2 chicks together so that they are about 5 or 6 inches apart. Then tie the pull cord to the front of the hen.

BABIES IN A BOAT

*T*hree babies in a boat
just bobbing around,
when one goes up
the other goes down. This
simple pull toy is an easy
project that you can make
over a weekend. It is de-
signed for children from
one to three years old.

A drill, a coping saw, and other ordinary hand tools are all that you need. You should have ⅛-inch, ¼-inch, ½-inch, and ⁹/₁₆-inch bits, a wood rasp, and several clamps. See the comments in Tools and Techniques on page 7.

Building Steps

1. Cut the hull from a piece of 2 by 4 that is about 12 to 14 inches long. This will give you enough wood to hold in a vise while cutting the shape. When cut out, the hull will be 9 inches long.

2. Trace the hull shape, both outside and inside, on the top of the 2 by 4. See Transferring Shapes From Illustrations on page 13. Drill a ¼-inch hole inside the center cutout area. Detach the blade from the coping saw, insert it through the hole, and reattach it. Carefully saw out the center cutout. Of course, you can make this cutout with a jigsaw or saber saw or with a scroll saw if you prefer.

3. Using a wood rasp, smooth the surfaces of this inside cutout. Finish sanding with sandpaper.

4. Next, cut the outside shape with a coping saw. Again, a saber saw, scroll saw, or even a band saw can also be used.

5. Smooth the outside (gunwales) with a rasp and sandpaper, sloping the sides slightly toward the bottom. Don't round the prow at this time. If you hold the hull in a vise for this, be sure to pad the jaws to prevent damage to the soft wood.

6. Now, using the hull as a pattern, trace the outside shape on a piece of ⅛-inch- to ¼-inch-thick wood for the bottom of the boat. Plywood or hardboard can be substituted if you cannot find a piece of solid wood. Cut this shape out.

7. Rip a piece 1 inch wide by about 8 inches long from a piece of ¾-inch-thick wood for the seats. Again, use the hull as a pattern: Mark the 3 seat locations. Place the hull on top of the seat stock and draw the inside pattern for the 3 seats. Cut out these 3 shapes, sawing on the outside of your lines so that they are slightly oversized.

8. The last piece to be cut is the axle block. Saw it from the ¾-inch-thick wood.

9. Holding the axle block in a vise (with padded jaws), drill a ¼-inch hole through the center. Be careful to keep this hole square and straight.

10. Cut 2 pieces of ⅛-inch dowel, ¾ inch long, for the movable-body stop pins. Put a piece of ½-inch dowel in the vise and saw the lengths as specified in the materials list for the 2 movable bodies and the stationary body. Using sandpaper, round one end of each of the 2 longer movable-body dowels. Lightly sand all the dowel pieces, removing fuzz and smoothing the surfaces.

11. Now start the assembly. Position the bottom carefully on the underside of the hull. Apply woodworking glue, and nail the bottom in place using the ¾-inch finishing brads. Keep the brads away from the bow, since you

Although not quite seaworthy, this little boat with its bobbing passengers makes a charming pull toy. There is even room for extra cargo between the babies.

Boat Hull Pattern on ½" Squares

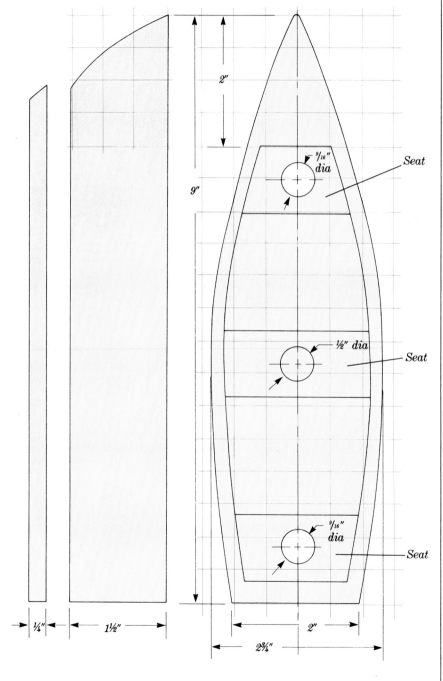

will be doing some additional shaping there. Use clamps to hold the 2 pieces tight. Place blocks of wood between the clamps and the work to spread the pressure and prevent mars. Wipe off any excess glue with a damp rag or sponge.

12. Check the fit of the 3 seat pieces in their correct locations. They will probably be somewhat oversized. Using a rasp and sandpaper, shape the seats until they fit snugly inside the boat hull. Apply glue and clamp in place.

13. The holes for the front and back babies are drilled all the way through the seat and bottom; the hole for the middle baby is not. This middle hole is called a blind hole.

Locate the center of the front and back seat and drill two $\frac{9}{16}$-inch holes down through the seat and out through the bottom. Put a piece of scrap wood under the boat to keep the drill bit from splitting the wood when it emerges.

Locate the center of the center seat. Drill a ½-inch hole, ¾ inch deep.

14. The three 1-inch wood balls are for the babies' heads. Drill ½-inch holes, ½ inch deep, into the center of (but not through) each. Take care to bore these holes straight toward the center. Next, drill a ⅛-inch hole through the dowels near the end of the 2 movable baby bodies, as shown in the illustrations. These are for the ⅛-inch stop pins.

15. Now smear a small amount of glue on the ends of the babies' bodies, and tap them into the holes in the wood-ball heads. Be careful not to use too much glue. The hydraulic pressure developed when driving in the dowels could split the balls. Wipe off any excess glue when done.

If for some reason the body dowels fit loosely in the holes, you can use rubber bands to hold the assembly together while the glue sets.

16. Go back to the hull and do the final shaping of this piece. Using a

wood rasp, shape the bow as shown in the illustration. Rasp and sand the bottom flush with the hull piece.

Fill any cracks or holes with the wood filler. Allow it to dry thoroughly, and then sand flush. Sand both the inside and the outside of the boat, starting with medium-grit sandpaper and finishing with fine-grit sandpaper. Round all the edges and remove all saw marks.

17. Next, attach the axle block to the bottom of the hull. Position it correctly, and glue and clamp it in place. Again, use blocks between the clamps and the toy. After the glue is dry, sand the axle block smooth and round the edges.

18. Apply a smear of glue on the end of the stationary (shorter) baby body, and tap it into the hole in the center seat.

After giving the movable babies a final sanding, slip them into the holes in the front and back seats. Glue and tap the ⅛-inch dowel stop pins into their holes in the baby-body dowels until centered. When the glue is dry, sand the ends of the pins round.

Note: You may want to paint the babies and the wheels a different color than the boat. If this is the case, don't install them until the painting is done.

19. Slip the 2 wheels onto the axle pegs. Apply a smear of glue to the ends of the pegs and tap them into the holes in the axle block. Don't tap so much that the wheels won't turn.

20. Give all the parts a final sanding, and dust them off well.

21. Finish by painting the boat a bright color, using a gloss enamel. You can either brush the paint on or use a spray enamel. Give the toy at least 2 coats.

Be careful not to use too much paint around the wheels. It can cause them to stick tight. Give the wheels a spin before the paint is fully set.

22. Attach the screw eye to the prow of the boat, tie on the pull cord, and you are ready to launch.

Boat Assembly

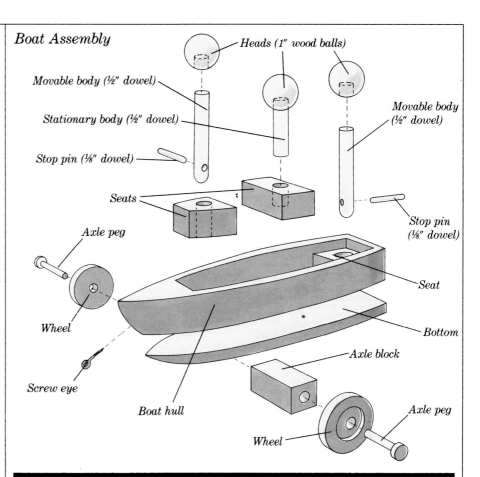

Materials List

You need short pieces of 1 by 4 and 2 by 4 lumber; a piece of ⅛-inch to ¼-inch solid wood, plywood, or hardboard material; and some hardwood dowels and balls to build this project. Try to find a soft, even-grained piece of 2 by 4, such as soft pine or spruce. It will make the hand-shaping easier.

Lumber

Piece	No. of Pieces	Thickness	Width	Length
Bottom	1	¼″	3½″	9″
Seats	3	¾″	1″	2½″
Axle block	1	¾″	¾″	2¾″
Hull	1	1½″	3½″	9″
Movable-body stop pins	2	⅛″ dowel		¾″
Movable bodies	2	½″ dowel		2½″
Stationary body	1	½″ dowel		1″

Hardware and Miscellaneous

Item	Quantity	Size	Description
Wood balls	3	1″ dia	Heads
Wood wheels	2	⅜″ × 2″ dia	With ¼″ axle holes
Axle pegs	2	¼″ × 1⅜″	
Wire brads	8	¾″	Finishing
Screw eye	1	3⁄16″ dia	For pull cord
Plastic cord	1	36″	
Wood filler	1 tube or small can		Matching wood color
Glue	1 small bottle		Woodworking
Sandpaper	2 sheets	100–150 grit	Medium and fine
Finish	1 can		Enamel or clear

WOBBLING GOOSE FAMILY

Mama goose and her two little goslings make a great Saturday project. You can build this project, with your little one- to three-year-old recipient looking on, in a matter of one or two hours. This is a simple project that can be built with basic hand tools.

All you need to cut the goose family shapes is a coping saw or, if you have one, a power jigsaw or scroll saw. A drill with ⅛-inch and ³/₁₆-inch bits and a wood rasp will finish the job.

Building Steps

1. Trace the outlines of the mother goose and the 2 goslings from the drawings, and transfer them to ¾-inch stock. See Transferring Shapes From Illustrations on page 13. Carefully cut out the shapes, using a coping saw, jigsaw, or scroll saw. Cut out the 2 goose wing blanks.

2. Mark the axle hole locations from the illustrations. Put a ³/₁₆-inch bit in the drill, and drill the axle holes through the 3 bodies. These should be straight and square.

3. Complete the parts by first smoothing all the edges with the wood rasp. With the rasp, shape the 2 wing parts to the edge pattern shown in the illustrations. The 2 wings are symmetrical, so they can be shaped identically. If you hold these pieces in a vise while rasping them, be sure to pad the vise jaws to avoid marring the pieces.

After you have obtained the desired wing shape, sand all the pieces. Round all the edges and corners and smooth the surfaces. Start with medium-grit sandpaper and progress to fine-grit sandpaper.

4. Cut the 3 axle dowels. Lightly sand them with fine-grit sandpaper after cutting to length. Don't overdo this on the ends of the axles—they must fit snugly into the wheel holes.

5. Finish all the parts before final assembly. Spray paint does a good job and saves much fuss and bother. A quick-drying enamel or lacquer also works well.

Goose Family Assembly

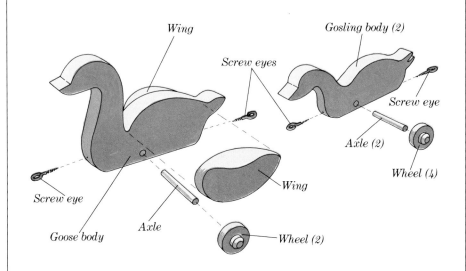

Wing · Screw eyes · Gosling body (2) · Screw eye · Axle (2) · Wheel (4) · Wing · Screw eye · Goose body · Axle · Wheel (2)

When pulling this toy, children will walk backward so that they can watch the action of these waddling geese.

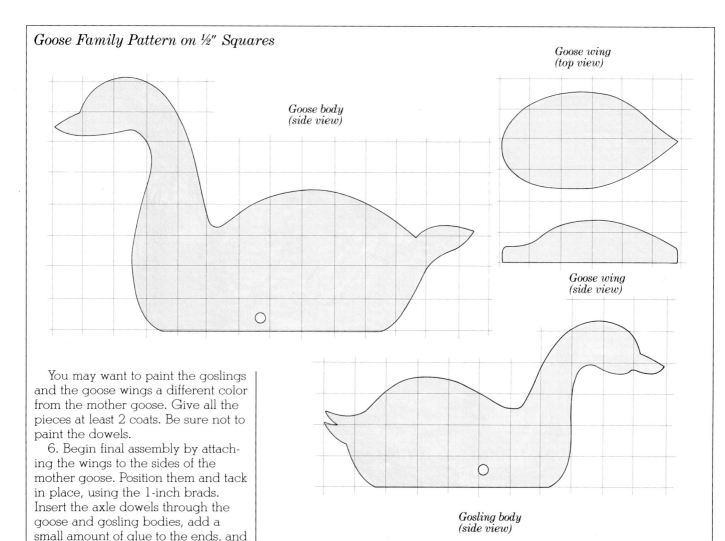

Goose Family Pattern on ½" Squares

Goose wing (top view)

Goose body (side view)

Goose wing (side view)

Gosling body (side view)

You may want to paint the goslings and the goose wings a different color from the mother goose. Give all the pieces at least 2 coats. Be sure not to paint the dowels.

6. Begin final assembly by attaching the wings to the sides of the mother goose. Position them and tack in place, using the 1-inch brads. Insert the axle dowels through the goose and gosling bodies, add a small amount of glue to the ends, and attach the wheels. Take care to insert or drive the dowels flush with the sides of the wheels. Wipe off any excess glue with a damp rag.

7. When everything is dry, you will probably want to touch up the bare dowel ends with matching paint. Spray some paint onto a piece of paper and use a small paintbrush to touch up the dowel ends. You may also elect to paint some trim with contrasting paint on the goose and gosling bodies, outlining their eyes, feathers, wings, and so on.

8. Note the locations of the screw eyes on the illustrations. Using the plastic cord, tie the mother goose and the 2 goslings together so that they are about 5 or 6 inches apart. Tie the pull cord to the front of the goose.

Materials List

Leftover pieces of soft pine, spruce, or soft hardwood such as alder or poplar, ¾ inch thick, would work well for this project. A piece of 1 by 6, 16 inches long, will do the job. The individual pieces should be reasonably clear. See Wood Materials, page 11.

Lumber

Piece	No. of Pieces	Thickness	Width	Length
Mother goose body	1	¾"	4½"	7"
Gosling bodies	2	¾"	2¾"	6"
Goose wings	2	¾"	1¾"	3"
Axles	3	⅛" dowel	1½"	

Hardware and Miscellaneous

Item	Quantity	Size	Description
Wood wheels	6	¼" × ¾" dia	Turned hardwood wheels
Wire brads	6	1"	Finishing
Screw eyes	3	⅛"	Bright, plated
Plastic cord	1	60"	
Glue	1 small bottle		Woodworking
Sandpaper	1–2 sheets	100–150 grit	Medium and fine
Finish	1 can		Enamel or lacquer

BALLS IN A CAGE

The wood balls in this push toy dance in the cage as your two- to four-year-old rolls it along. The hollow wooden sound of the bouncing balls is far more pleasant than the clicking and snapping of many commercial toys on the market today.

You need a coping saw, jigsaw, or band saw for cutting all the round or curved pieces. A drill press facilitates the boring of the dowel holes. The other tools needed include basic hand tools, a drill with a ⅛-inch, ¼-inch, ¹⁷⁄₆₄-inch, ⅜-inch, and ¾-inch bits, and C-clamps for the assembly. See the comments in Tools and Techniques on page 7.

Building Steps

1. Cut out the 4 inner and outer circle blanks. Cut two 8½-inch squares from the ¼-inch plywood and two 8½-inch squares from the ⅛-inch plywood or hardboard.

2. Stack these 4 pieces, keeping the thicknesses paired, and tack them together temporarily, using one of the techniques described in Duplicate Sawing or Drilling on page 9. Brads or double-stick tape would work well in this application. Arrange the pieces so that the outside grain of the ¼-inch plywood is perpendicular to that of the ⅛-inch plywood. Draw diagonal lines from the corners to locate the center of the top piece, and draw an 8-inch circle using a drawing compass. Now, using a coping saw, jigsaw, or band saw, carefully cut the circles.

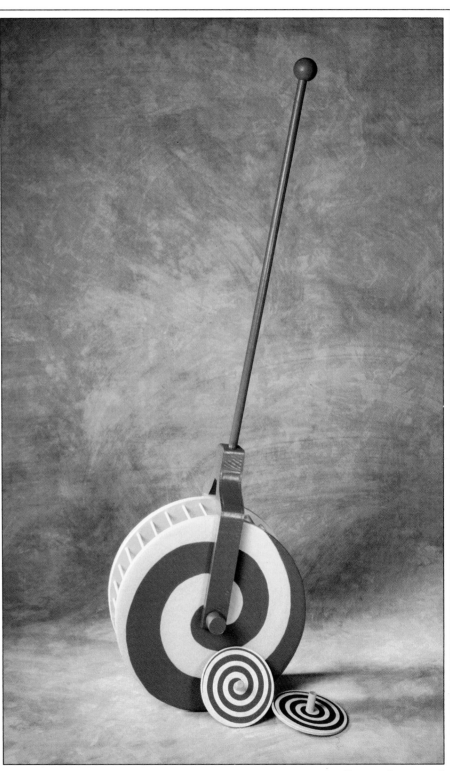

This little push or pull toy makes enough noise to appeal to a youngster, and when painted with spirals on the outside, as shown, it is fascinating to watch as it rolls along.

Cage Side Pattern on ½" Squares

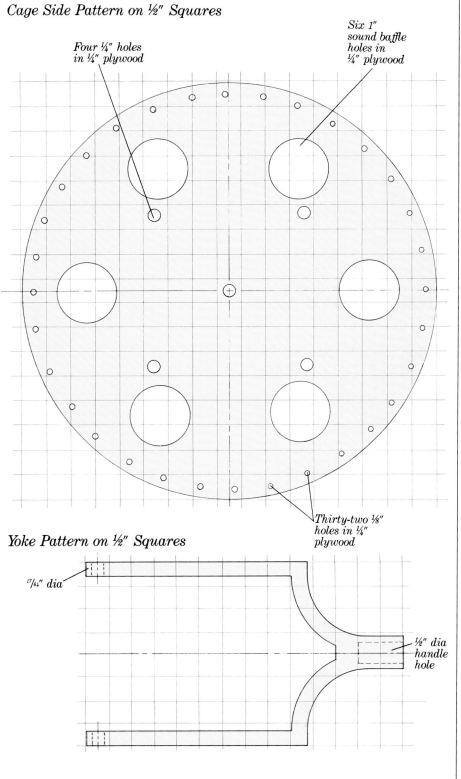

Four ¼" holes in ¼" plywood

Six 1" sound baffle holes in ¼" plywood

Thirty-two ⅛" holes in ¼" plywood

Yoke Pattern on ½" Squares

¹⁷⁄₆₄" dia

½" dia handle hole

3. While the stack is still together, drill a ¹⁷⁄₆₄-inch hole down through the center. Use a drill press, if one is available. Otherwise, be sure to keep this hole square and straight. Use a piece of scrap wood under the stack to prevent the drill from splitting the wood when it emerges.

Next, mark the location of the six 1-inch-diameter sound baffle holes (see illustration). Drill these holes. Use a spur or Forstner-type bit, if available. Spade bits tend to tear when entering plywood. Again, use a piece of scrap wood for backup.

4. Now sand the outside edges of the stack. Do the final shaping of the circle and remove all saw marks. A good way to do this, if you have a stationary disk or belt sander, is to put a piece of ¼-inch dowel through the center hole and then, holding the axle stationary, rotate the edges against the sander. When done, put a reference pencil mark across the edges so that you can align the disks again later.

5. Separate the ¼-inch and ⅛-inch pairs. Next, you will be drilling a total of thirty-six holes for the cage dowels in the ¼-inch-thick plywood pieces. Leave the pairs tacked together. If possible, use a drill press for these holes, as they need to be perfectly straight and square. If a drill press is not available, a commercial drill guide will do the job. Otherwise, do the best you can by hand. As before, use a piece of scrap wood for backup.

Lay out the locations for the four ¼-inch and thirty-two ⅛-inch holes. Drill the holes. Note: You might want to practice first on a piece of scrap to see what drill speed and pressure give the cleanest holes.

6. Cut all the dowel pieces to length. Start by cutting the ¼-inch cage axle and the four ¼-inch inner cage dowels to length. Cut the handle from a piece of ½-inch dowel.

Cage Assembly

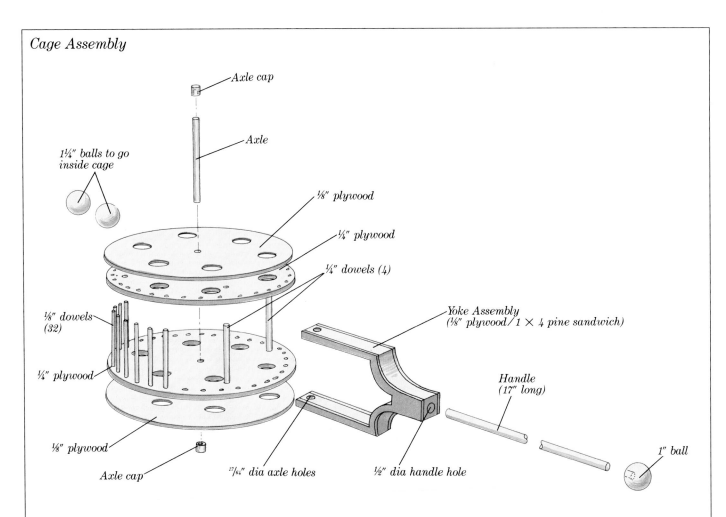

Axle cap

Axle

1¼" balls to go inside cage

⅛" plywood

¼" plywood

¼" dowels (4)

Yoke Assembly
(⅛" plywood / 1 × 4 pine sandwich)

⅛" dowels (32)

Handle (17" long)

¼" plywood

⅛" plywood

Axle cap

¹⁷⁄₆₄" dia axle holes

½" dia handle hole

1" ball

Make the axle caps by putting a 3- to 4-inch length of ½-inch dowel in the vise. Drill a ¼-inch hole in the center of each end ⅝ inch deep. Now cut a ¾-inch piece off each end of this dowel. These are the axle caps.

Cut the 32 outer cage dowels. Since there are so many and the lengths need to be the same, it would be a good idea to rig up some sort of jig or stop to cut these pieces, whether you are cutting by hand or with a power saw. Cut an extra piece or two while you are doing this.

Cutting short dowels with a power saw, especially a table saw, can be tricky and possibly dangerous. Fingers get very close to the revolving blades. The saw can easily catch the dowel, spin it out of your fingers,

and throw it. Be careful not to allow the short dowel pieces to become trapped between the fence or stop and the saw blade. They can be thrown toward you at high speed.

7. Now begin the assembly. While the glue is drying, you can work on some of the other parts.

Separate all 4 circles. Lightly sand the faces to remove any fuzz or raised grain. Glue each outer side to an inner side piece, using your marks for alignment. Restack and clamp the 2 pairs together. Use blocks to spread the pressure and keep the clamps from marring the surface. Be sure to

clean off any excess glue with a wet rag or sponge to keep the 2 pairs from sticking together.

8. While the glue is drying, saw the square yoke blanks. The yoke center is cut from ¾-inch stock, the outer yoke pieces from the ⅛-inch plywood or hardboard.

9. Face-glue the yoke pieces, sandwiching the thick piece between the 2 thin pieces. Clamp together, again using blocks between the clamps and the piece.

10. While that piece is drying, return to the 2 cage side assemblies. Separate them and give these pieces a thorough sanding, rounding all the edges and smoothing the faces. Sand away any dried glue. Be careful not to sand away your reference marks.

Take all the cage dowels, both ⅛ inch and ¼ inch, and give each a light sanding, removing fuzz and smoothing them. Also sand the two 1½-inch wood balls at this time, if they need it.

Note: You may want to consider painting the cage balls different colors. Now is the time to do so. Once they are dry, put the balls in a light plastic bag when you put them in the cage to shield them from the final finish. Remove the bag after you finish the cage.

11. Put the cage pieces together by first laying one side assembly flat on a workbench. Apply a small amount of glue to the ends of each of the dowels, and tap them into their respective holes.

Put the 2 balls in the open cage now. Once the other side is glued in place, there is no turning back.

Set the other side on top of the open cage and align the reference marks. Again, using a small amount of glue either on the ends of the dowels or in the holes, tap the side down until all the dowels are firmly bottomed in their respective holes. If necessary, clamp the 2 sides together until the glue has set.

12. Unclamp the yoke assembly, and draw the yoke pattern on the top. See Transferring Shapes From Illustrations on page 13. This would be a good time to drill the ¹⁷/₆₄-inch axle holes and the ½-inch blind handle hole. Check the illustrations for the hole locations. The handle hole is 1½ inches deep, and the axle holes should be at least ¾ inch deep. As with the previous holes, these all need to be square and straight.

While you have the ½-inch drill bit handy, drill a blind hole into the center of the 1-inch ball for the end of the handle.

Materials List

Plywood is the principal material for this toy. One-quarter-inch plywood is used for the insides of the cage, and ⅛-inch plywood is used for the outside. Birch or a hardwood plywood is preferred for both, although you could use ¼-inch AC-grade softwood plywood for the insides.

If you have a difficult time finding ⅛-inch plywood, you can substitute ⅛-inch hardboard or even ¼-inch plywood for the outside pieces of the cage. A 9- by 18-inch piece of the ¼-inch plywood and a 9- by 26-inch piece of the ⅛-inch thickness are needed for the project. Note that if you substitute the ¼-inch plywood for the outer sides, the yoke assembly parts will have to be cut ¼ inch wider.

A small piece of ¾-inch pine is required for the yoke. Other materials needed include approximately 8 feet of ⅛-inch hardwood dowel, 1½ feet of ¼-inch dowel, and 2 feet of ½-inch dowel. The wood balls should also be hardwood. See Wood Materials, page 11.

Lumber

Piece	No. of Pieces	Thickness	Width	Length
Outer sides	2	⅛″ plywood	8½″	8½″
Outer yoke pieces	2	⅛″ plywood	4″	7″
Inner sides	2	¼″ plywood	8½″	8½″
Yoke center	1	¾″	4″	7″
Outer cage	32	⅛″ dowel	2¾″	
Inner cage	4	¼″ dowel	2¾″	
Axle	1	¼″ dowel	4″	
Handle	1	½″ dowel	17″	
Axle caps	2	½″ dowel	¾″	

Hardware and Miscellaneous

Item	Quantity	Size	Description
Wood ball	1	1″ dia	For handle
Wood balls	2	1½″ dia	For cage
Wire brads	20	1″	Finishing
Wood filler	1 tube or small can		Matching wood color
Glue	1 small bottle		Woodworking
Sandpaper	2–3 sheets	100–150 grit	Medium and fine
Finish	1 can		Enamel or clear

13. Now saw out the yoke shape using a coping saw or a band saw with a narrow blade.

14. Give all the pieces associated with the handle assembly a sanding, removing all saw marks, rounding the edges, and smoothing the surfaces. Sand all the dowel parts, including the axle and axle caps.

15. Assemble the handle by gluing the handle into the yoke at one end and into the ball handle at the other. Finally, slide the axle dowel through the side of the yoke, the cage sides, and the other side of the yoke. Glue the axle caps in place.

16. To finish the project, give all the parts a final sanding—especially where glue has smeared. Then dust them off well.

If you have used an attractive plywood and prefer a natural finish, a clear satin polyurethane varnish or lacquer would look attractive. If you do this, you may want to add some color trim. You could also use an enamel paint. In any case, spray paint is preferable for a project of this size. It is easy to apply, and cleanup is minimal. Be sure to read the instructions on the can carefully. Give all parts at least 2 coats of finish.

SUPER RACERS

These racers are quick projects that take little time but create a lot of excitement. You can make one or all in a weekend. The gleam in your two- to six-year-old's eyes will be reward enough for making all three.

All of these Super Racer toys can be built with basic hand-held tools: You need a jigsaw, a coping saw, a drill with ¼-inch and ¹⁷⁄₃₂-inch bits, a wood rasp, several C-clamps, and a small chisel. The ¼-inch bit should be brad pointed. The availability of certain stationary power tools would facilitate the construction of these attractive toys. You could use a band saw or scroll saw for the curved cuts, a table or radial arm saw for the straight cuts, and a power sander for final shaping and finishing. A drill press would be very handy, especially with the drag racer. See the comments in Tools and Techniques on page 7.

Flying Wing Racer

Building Steps

1. Begin by cutting the piece of 2 by 4 to length. Because the racer shape is curved in both planes, it will be easier to make the rear axle cutout when the piece is still square. Draw the lines for this cutout on the side of the piece and saw it out. Use a handsaw or any power saw for this. A table or radial arm saw with a dado blade will work well.

2. Draw the top and side body shapes on the piece. See Transferring Shapes From Illustrations on page 13. Saw out the top shape. Saw carefully to save shaping and sanding later.

Using tape or several small drops of hot-melt adhesive, reattach the 2 pieces just removed so that the piece

Flying Wing Racer Assembly

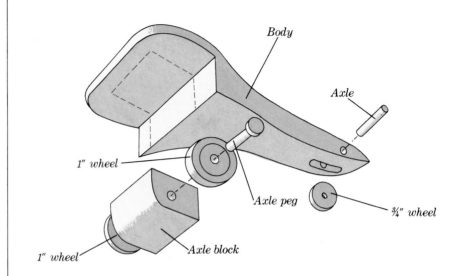

- Body
- Axle
- 1" wheel
- Axle peg
- ¾" wheel
- 1" wheel
- Axle block

Easy to make and fun to paint, this Flying Wing Racer has the look of a jet but speeds along on three wheels.

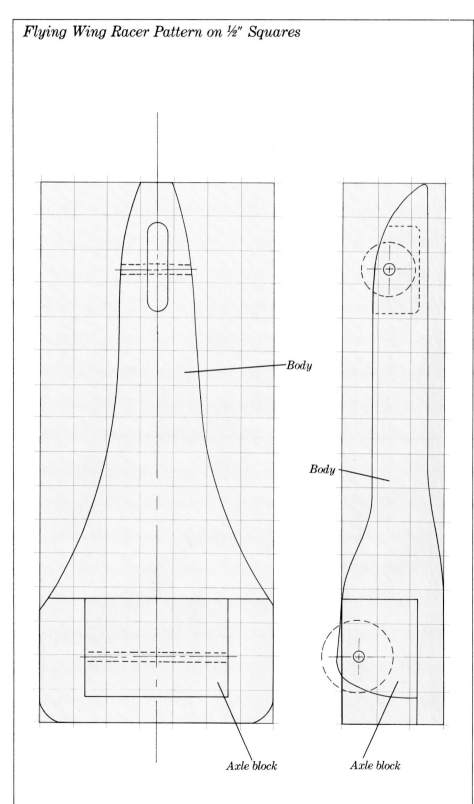

Body

Body

Axle block

Axle block

is again square. Then saw out the side profile. Use a coping saw or band saw for these cuts. If the piece is in a metal-jawed vise, be sure to pad the jaws to avoid damaging the surfaces.

3. Cut the axle block to size. You can use the cutout piece sawn in step 1 or any other scrap you have. Shape and round one end as shown in the illustrations.

4. Now you need to make a recess in the front of the racer for the front wheel. Using the illustrations as a guide, first draw a centerline and then draw out the shape of this recess on the bottom of the piece.

Carefully drill a row of three or four ¼-inch holes, ½ inch deep. Use a stop with the drill bit to control this depth. The overall length of the recess is about 1 inch. If possible, use a brad-pointed bit to keep the bit from skating or shifting when starting the entrance hole. Clean out and square the sides of this slot with a chisel.

5. Locate the position for the axle hole from the illustrations, and drill a ⅛-inch hole for the front axle. Do the same in the rear axle block.

6. Position the axle block in the racer-body cutout, apply woodworking glue, and clamp in place. Use pads between the clamps and your work to prevent marring.

7. Smooth and finalize the shape of the Flying Wing Racer with a wood rasp. Follow with sanding, progressing from medium- to fine-grit sandpaper. The smoother the final surface, the better the finished racer will look.

8. If you want to paint the wheels a different color than the racer body, skip the next 2 steps and install the painted wheels after final finishing.

9. Cut a 1⅛-inch piece of ⅛-inch dowel for the front axle. Sand it until it slips easily (but still snugly) in and out of the front axle hole. Slip it through the ¾-inch front wheel. Make sure the wheel turns freely. If it doesn't, make any necessary enlargements to the front-wheel recess with your chisel.

When ready, reinsert the axle through the body and wheel, and glue it in place. Make sure no glue gets into the axle/wheel area. Give the wheel a spin occasionally while the glue sets to keep it free. Sand the dowel ends flush with the body after the glue has dried.

10. To install the rear wheels, slip the wheels onto the axle pegs, apply a smear of glue to the ends of the pegs, and tap them into the holes in the rear axle block.

11. That completes the racer. Give it a final sanding and then finish it. If you used an attractive wood, you may elect to use a clear finish such as varnish, lacquer, or wax. A bright high-gloss enamel would also look good, in which case you can either brush it on or use spray paint. Spray finish is the easiest to apply and clean up. See Finishing on page 11 for more information.

Give the Flying Wing Racer at least 2 coats of finish. Be careful not to overpaint around the wheels or they will stick. After the finish is fully dried, a coat of paste wax, buffed to a gloss, will make the racer look sharp.

Ball-Wheel Racer

Building Steps

1. Cut the piece of 1½-inch stock to size for the racer body. Transfer and enlarge both the top and the side shapes from the illustration to the surface of the piece. See Transferring Shapes From Illustrations on page 13.

While the piece is still square, drill the 2 axle holes. Mark the locations from the drawings. These holes are $^{17}/_{64}$ inch in diameter so that the ¼-inch dowel axles will turn freely. The holes need to be square and straight. Use a drill press if possible.

2. Saw out the top body profile, using a coping saw, band saw, or scroll saw. Saw carefully along the lines, saving the scrap pieces.

Reattach the 2 scrap pieces, using tape or small drops of hot-melt adhesive to return the piece to its square shape. Now saw the side body profile. Separate the scrap pieces, scraping off any adhesive (if used).

Materials List

A short piece of 2 by 4 lumber is all you need for the Flying Wing Racer. Try to find a piece of a soft, even-grained wood, such as white pine or spruce. It will make the hand-shaping easier. If you like simple but attractive hardwood toys with a natural finish, birch, hard maple, alder, or cherry are good choices for this project, but they are more difficult to shape.

If you cannot find a piece 1½ inches thick in the wood of your choice, you can face-glue 2 pieces of ¾-inch stock together for the racer body. For more information on selecting wood and gluing, see Wood Materials, page 11, and Gluing, page 10.

Lumber

Piece	No. of Pieces	Thickness	Width	Length
Racer body	1	1½"	3½"	8"
Axle	1	⅛" dowel	1⅛"	

Hardware and Miscellaneous

Item	Quantity	Size	Description
Wood wheel	1	¾" dia	With ⅛" axle hole
Wood wheels	2	1" dia	With ⅛" axle holes
Axle pegs	2	⅛" × 1⅛"	
Glue	1 small bottle		Woodworking
Sandpaper	2 sheets	100–150 grit	Medium and fine
Finish	1 can		Enamel or clear
Paste wax	Small amount		

This stylized racer, suitable for the Grand Prix, has enlarged wheels for fast getaways.

Ball Wheel Racer Pattern on ½" Squares   *Ball Wheel Racer Assembly*

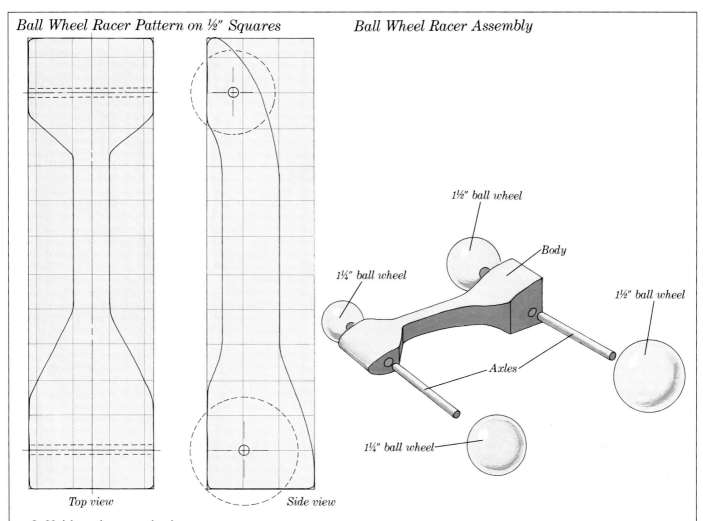

Top view   Side view

1½" ball wheel

Body

1¼" ball wheel

1½" ball wheel

Axles

1¼" ball wheel

3. Holding the racer body in a padded vise, rasp the final shape smooth. Use medium-grit then fine-grit sandpaper to remove all saw marks, round all the edges, and smooth all the surfaces.

4. Drill ¼-inch holes to the center of the 4 wood balls. Take care in doing this, making sure the holes are properly aligned and centered. Otherwise, you will get a wobble when the ball wheels are installed.

5. Cut the two ¼-inch axle dowels to length. Lightly sand them smooth.

6. Insert the axles through the axle holes, and glue the balls on the ends. Check for free rotation, and adjust if necessary before the glue sets.

7. Give the racer a final sanding and dust it off. Finish the racer using paint or clear finish. See step 11 of the Flying Wing Racer for details.

Materials List

Again, a short piece of 2 by 4 lumber is all that is needed for the Ball-Wheel Racer project. See the comments in the materials list for the Flying Wing Racer.

Lumber

Piece	No. of Pieces	Thickness	Width	Length
Racer body	1	1½"	1¾"	6¼"
Axles	2	¼" dowel	3"	

Hardware and Miscellaneous

Item	Quantity	Size	Description
Wood balls	2	1¼" dia	Front wheels
Wood balls	2	1½" dia	Rear wheels
Glue	1 small bottle		Woodworking
Sandpaper	2 sheets	100–150 grit	Medium and fine
Finish	1 can		Enamel or clear
Paste wax	Small amount		

Drag Racer

Building Steps

1. Cut the body blank from the 1 by 4. Transfer the inside and outside shapes from the illustrations to the piece. See Transferring Shapes From Illustrations on page 13.

2. While the body is still in a squared shape, drill the axle holes. Mark the hole locations on the side. Using a ¼-inch drill bit, bore the holes, taking care to keep them square and straight.

3. To make the trapezoidal cutout in the front of the racer, drill a ¼-inch saw-blade entrance hole. Then detach the blade on a coping or scroll saw, insert it through the hole, reattach it, and saw the cutout. A saber saw or jigsaw can also be used for making this inside cut.

Next, saw out the outside shape of the racer body. Sand all the sawn edges smooth, removing saw marks and rounding edges.

4. Copy the motor-block shape onto a piece of ¾-inch-thick 1 by 4 material. Cut this piece to shape, using either a handsaw or power saw. Sand all its surfaces smooth, and round the top and side edges.

5. Do the same with the seat. A coping or scroll saw is needed to make the curved shapes.

6. Finally, make the motor cowling. This is cut from a scrap of 1 by 4. Use the shape shown or a more square shape of your own design.

7. From the ¼-inch dowel stock, cut 12 top cylinders and 12 side cylinders to the lengths shown in the materials list. You may want to rig up a simple jig or stop arrangement so that each set of dowels is the same length. Lightly sand all these dowels to remove fuzz and smooth surfaces.

Saw the driver body from a ¼-inch dowel. Cut the short steering-wheel post from a piece of ⅛-inch dowel, and sand both smooth.

8. Using a drill or drill press, bore the blind cylinder holes in the motor block. They are ¼ inch in diameter and ¼ inch deep. Carefully mark the location for the 12 top and side holes. Use a brad-pointed drill bit, if possible, to ensure the most accurately located holes.

The drill press, if you have one, is the best tool to use for this, but you are going to have to clamp a little jig on the table to permit the side holes to be drilled perpendicular to the center axis. Refer to the illustration for details on the hole locations and direction. When done, sand off any splinters or fuzz.

9. Finish the drilling by boring a blind ¼-inch hole in the bottom of the seat. Drill the same size hole into the center of the 1-inch ball. Drill a ⅛-inch blind hole in the dash portion of the seat for the steering post. Make all three of these holes ½ inch deep.

Drag Racer Assembly

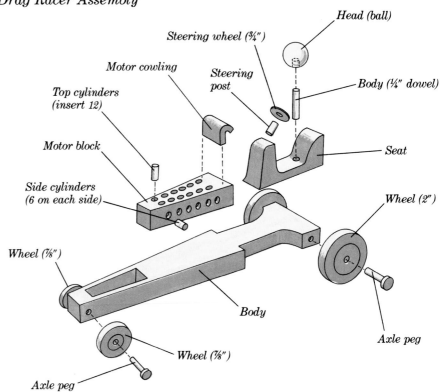

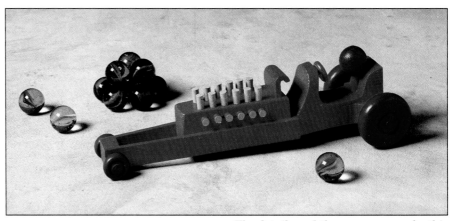

The details and the passenger make this Drag Racer all the more fun.

Drag Racer Pattern on ½" Squares

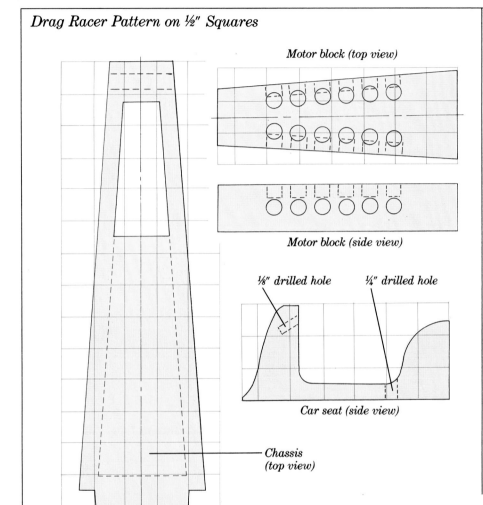

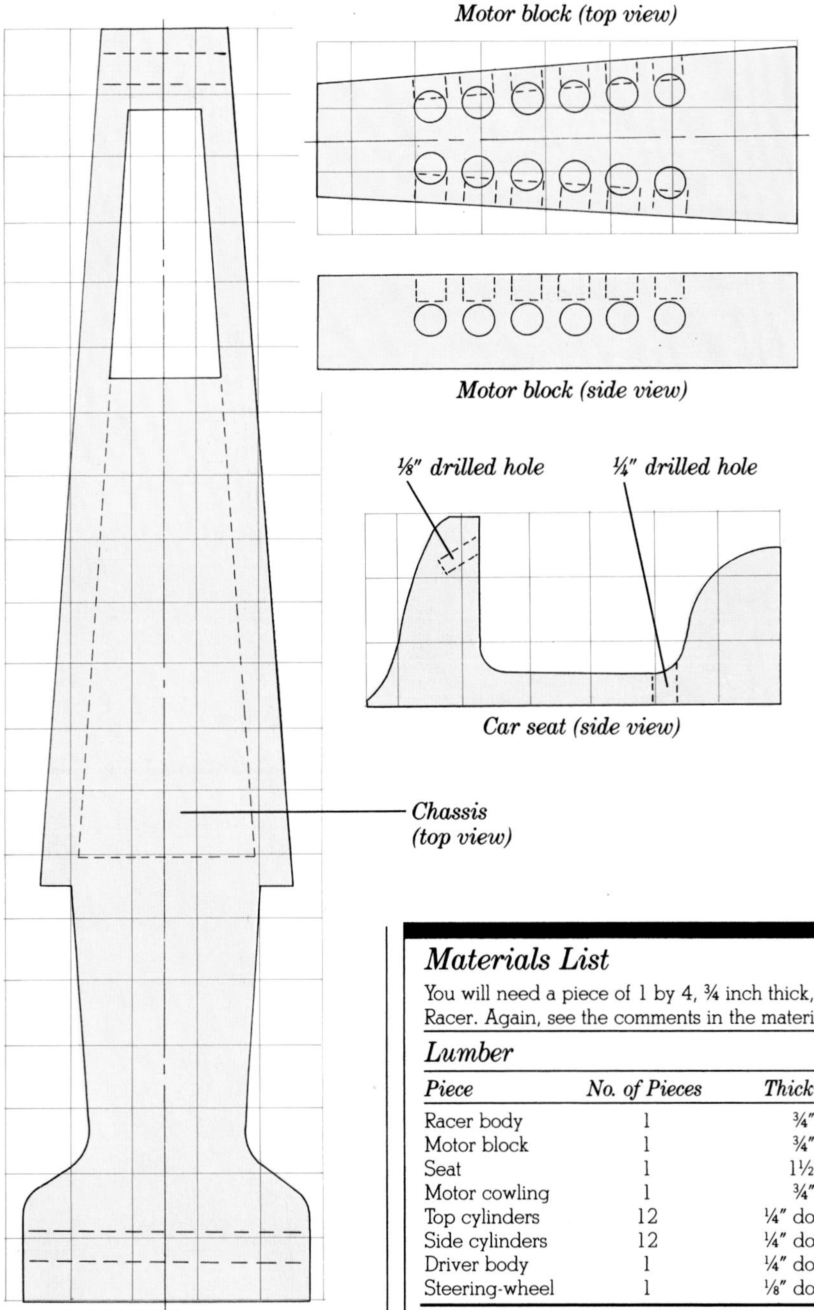

Motor block (top view)

Motor block (side view)

⅛" drilled hole

¼" drilled hole

Car seat (side view)

Chassis
(top view)

Motor Cowling Pattern on ¼" Squares

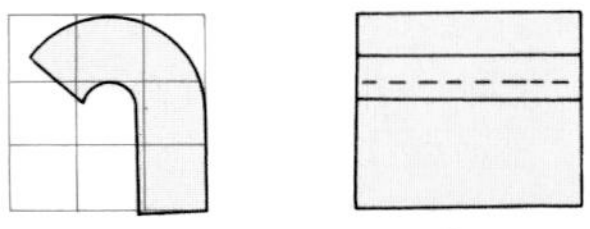

Side view   Back view

10. Begin the assembly by inserting the dowel cylinders in the motor block and gluing them in place. Take care not to use too much glue, or hydraulic pressure can develop when the dowels are introduced, and the piece may split. Use only a smear of glue, or carve a slight flat on the side of the dowel to allow excess glue to escape. Wipe off any excess glue with a damp rag when done.

11. Glue the motor block and the seat in place. Use C-clamps to hold the pieces tightly in position while the glue dries. Pad the clamps to avoid marring the work. When dry, glue the motor cowling in place.

12. Glue and insert the driver-body dowel in its hole in the seat. Apply glue to the other end and tap the driver-head ball onto it. Finish by assembling the steering wheel in the same way. The ¾-inch-diameter wheel is used for this.

13. Finally, attach the wheels. Slip the ⅞-inch front wheels and the 2-inch rear wheels onto the 4 axle pegs and then glue them into the axle holes. Be sure all 4 wheels turn freely.

14. After a final sanding, you can finish the racer. Refer to step 11 of the Flying Wing Racer for a discussion of finishing.

Materials List

You will need a piece of 1 by 4, ¾ inch thick, and a piece of 2 by 4, 1½ inches thick, for this Drag Racer. Again, see the comments in the materials list for the Flying Wing Racer.

Lumber

Piece	No. of Pieces	Thickness	Width	Length
Racer body	1	¾"	3"	10"
Motor block	1	¾"	1½"	3¾"
Seat	1	1½"	1½"	3¼"
Motor cowling	1	¾"	¾"	1"
Top cylinders	12	¼" dowel		¾"
Side cylinders	12	¼" dowel		½"
Driver body	1	¼" dowel		1½"
Steering-wheel	1	⅛" dowel		1"

Hardware and Miscellaneous

Item	Quantity	Size	Description
Wood wheel	1	¾" dia	With ⅛" axle hole
Wood wheels	2	⅞" dia	With ¼" axle holes
Wood wheels	2	2" dia	With ¼" axle holes
Wood ball	1	1" dia	Driver's head
Axle pegs	4	¼" × 1⅜"	
Glue	1 small bottle		Woodworking
Sandpaper	2 sheets	100–150 grit	Medium and fine
Finish	1 can		Enamel or clear

NOAH'S ARK

This pull toy will store all the little animals as your two- to four-year-old pulls it through the house. It may not survive the great flood, but it will bring hours of enjoyment. This is a fairly straightforward project to build and should be a weekend workshop project.

You will need a jigsaw or band saw to make the curved hull parts. A coping saw, scroll saw, or band saw with a very narrow blade is needed for cutting out the animal shapes. A table or radial arm saw will help in making the straight and angled saw cuts and will ensure that the pieces fit together well. Other tool requirements include ⅛-inch, ¼-inch, and ½-inch drill bits, a wood rasp, some C-clamps, and ordinary hand tools. See the comments in Tools and Techniques on page 7.

Building Steps

1. To start this project, lay out all the pieces to be cut from the ¼-inch plywood. To do this, transfer the shapes from the illustrations to pieces of thin cardboard or poster board. See Transferring Shapes From Illustrations on page 13. Cut out the shapes with scissors or a board knife and then move the shapes around on the piece of plywood to get the most efficient use of the material.

2. Begin sawing out the house parts. You will probably want to rough-cut these pieces with a jigsaw or band saw and then saw them to final dimension on the table or radial arm saw. Cut each roof piece, the 2 sides of the house, and the house front and back blanks. Make sure all the cuts are square and straight. Use a special plywood blade or a smooth-cut cabinet saw blade to minimize the tearing of the edge grain.

Saw the pointed rooflines of the front and back pieces with a table saw miter gauge or radial arm saw, set to 35 or 55 degrees respectively. Cut out the door opening in the front piece with a jigsaw or band saw.

3. Loosely assemble all the house pieces to make sure everything is cut correctly and fits. Check the drawings to be sure positioning is correct.

Give the flat surfaces a good sanding. Progress from medium-grit to fine-grit sandpaper. Fill any open voids in the visible plywood edges with wood filler. Sand flush when dry.

4. Start the assembly by using the ⅝-inch finishing brads and the woodworking glue to attach the front and back to the sides of the house. Glue and nail the 2 roof pieces in place. Wipe away any excess glue with a damp rag or sponge.

When the glue has dried, give the assembled house a final sanding. Sand the roof joint at the peak so that it is flush, round all the edges and corners, sand away any saw marks, and smooth the surfaces. This completes the ark house.

5. Study the illustrations of the hull so that you understand the construction. It consists of a plywood bottom, 2 hull wall pieces, and rails on top. Transfer the 2 hull wall shapes

Whether it's rolling across the sea or docked to let the animals roam, this ark is sure to provide hours of entertainment.

to pieces of 2 by 6 lumber. See Transferring Shapes From Illustrations on page 13. Try to avoid any large knots or other defects in the wood. Saw the hull wall pieces out, using a jigsaw or band saw. Use a fine-tooth saw blade. Saw carefully and smoothly; it will save sanding later.

6. Retrieve the piece of ¼-inch plywood with the patterns for the hullbottom and rails. Rough-saw the blanks for these shapes. Carefully saw the hull bottom.

The 2 hull rail pieces can be cut to shape together by doubling up the 2 plywood blanks. Refer to Duplicate Sawing or Drilling on page 9 for suggestions on joining pieces temporarily.

Again, saw carefully to minimize final sanding.

7. From a small piece of the 2 by 6, rip the 2 axle blocks. This will require 2 rip passes to reach the required dimensions. First, rip off two ¾-inch-thick pieces, and then rerip to the 1⅛-inch width. If you are doing this on a table saw, be sure to use a push stick and a hold-down, and watch your fingers. Cut to final length.

With a jigsaw or band saw, cut out the notches in the 2 axle blocks, as shown in the drawings.

8. As you did before, preassemble all the parts to check their fit. Sand the flat surfaces of the bottom, the inside faces of the hull walls, and the rails to remove all saw marks; smooth the

curves. A drum sander would work well for this, if available. Sand the faces of the axle blocks smooth, but don't round the corners.

9. Start the hull assembly by nailing and gluing the 2 hull wall pieces to the bottom. You may need to use clamps. Be sure to pad them to avoid marring the pieces. Wipe off any excess glue. After the glue has dried, fill any voids or cracks with wood filler. Sand flush the outside curves, the joint between the hull bottom, and the walls. A stationary belt sander works well for this.

10. Attach the rail pieces, wiping off any excess glue. After the glue has dried, fill any voids in the plywood. When dry, sand the filler flush. Sand the outside curve of the rail smooth, and round all the edges.

11. Before attaching the axle blocks to the bottom of the hull, drill the ¼-inch axle holes through the blocks. Carefully locate the holes. The alignment is important here, or the axle dowels will not fit.

12. Cut the two ¼-inch axle dowels to length. Sand them lightly. Slide them through the holes in the axle blocks. If needed, reshape the holes, using a small rat-tail or chain-saw file. You want a free but snug fit.

13. Next, attach the axle blocks to the bottom of the hull, positioning them as shown in the illustrations. You will be nailing down through the hull bottom into the blocks, so you may want to locate the nail holes carefully with a light pencil mark. Apply glue and position the blocks on the bottom. Nail together, using 3 brads in each axle block.

14. Give the axle blocks a final sanding to round the edges and corners. Apply some glue on the center of the axle dowels and slide them into the axle blocks. Make sure the axles are centered before the glue sets. Wipe away any excess glue.

15. Drill a carefully centered ¼-inch hole in the end of a short piece of

Ark Pattern—Animals on 1″ Squares

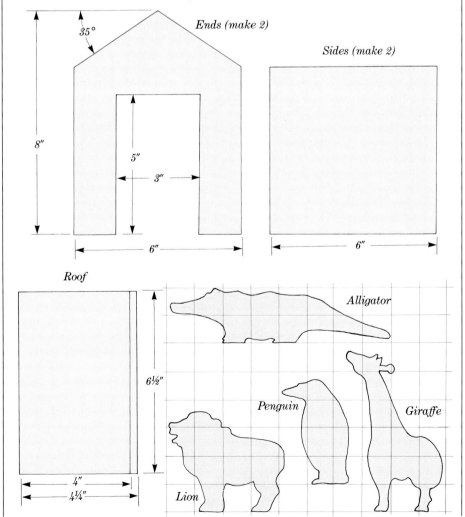

35

½-inch dowel. Drill at least ⅜ inch deep. Saw off an axle hub piece ⅜ inch long. Do this 3 more times to give you the 4 hubs needed.

16. Drill a ⁹⁄₁₆-inch axle hole in the center of each wheel, if you haven't done so already. Slip the wheels on the axles, making sure they turn freely. Glue the hubs on the ends of the axles to hold the wheels in place.

17. Since the animal shapes are in pairs, cut both shapes at once. See Duplicate Sawing and Drilling on page 9. A coping or scroll saw is best for cutting these shapes, but you can also use a jigsaw or band saw equipped with a very narrow blade.

Finish the animal shapes by rasping, if necessary, and sanding the edges and surfaces smooth. Slightly round all the corners.

18. Now go back to the power saw and rip the stock for the animal stands. Take the same precautions you used when ripping the axle blocks. Cut the stands to varying lengths to fit the 4 different animals. Sand smooth. The animals will stand better if you sand the bottom of the base at a slight angle so that they tilt backward slightly. See the illustrations for details.

19. Glue and clamp a base to each animal. After the glue has dried, give each animal a final sanding.

20. Before finishing the toy, give all the parts a final light sanding and blow off all dust.

You will probably want to use a bright, glossy enamel paint. Use your imagination. All the parts should have at least 2 coats. Using a good primer will help hide some of the strong plywood grain.

Spray paint works well for small objects like this ark and its passengers. If you do use a spray finish, be sure to use it in a well-ventilated location and follow the directions on the can. Be careful not to get too much paint on the wheels and axles or they will stick. Give each wheel a spin before the finish has set.

21. Screw the screw eye into the ark's prow and attach the pull cord. Noah's Ark is ready for a flood.

Hull Pattern on 1" Squares

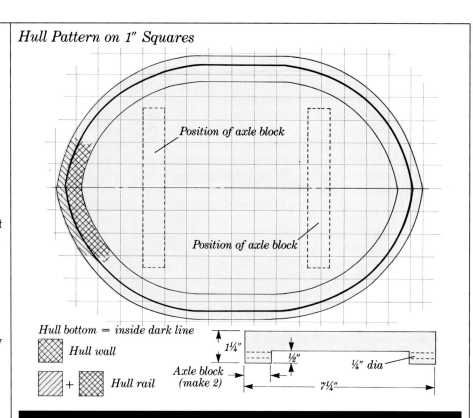

Position of axle block

Position of axle block

Hull bottom = inside dark line

▨ Hull wall

▨ + ▨ Hull rail

Axle block (make 2)

1¼" ½" ¼" dia 7¼"

Materials List

The Noah's Ark Pull Toy can be built out of common softwood. Use ¼-inch AC-grade plywood. Birch or other hardwood can also be used. The solid lumber parts come from common 2 by 6 material, 1½ inches thick. Choose a soft-textured wood such as soft pine or spruce. See Wood Materials, page 11.

You are going to need approximately 2 by 3 feet of plywood and 3 feet of 2 by 6 lumber. The dowels should be hardwood.

Lumber

Piece	No. of Pieces	Thickness	Width	Length
House roof	1	¼" plywood	4¼"	7"
House roof	1	¼" plywood	4"	7"
House sides	2	¼" plywood	6"	6"
House front and back	2	¼" plywood	6"	8"
Hull rails	2	¼" plywood	6"	16½"
Hull sides	2	1½"	5½"	16"
Hull bottom	1	¼" plywood	11"	15¾"
Animal shapes	8	¼" plywood	2"–4"	4"–8"
Animal stands	8	⅜"	½"	1½"–3"
Axle blocks	2	¾"	1⅛"	4¼"
Axles	2	¼" dowel	8¾"	
Axle hubs	4	½" dowel	¾"	

Hardware and Miscellaneous

Item	Quantity	Size	Description
Wood wheels	4	⁷⁄₁₆" × 1¼"	With ⁹⁄₁₆" axle holes
Wire brads	30	⅝"	Finishing
Plastic cord	1	36"	
Screw eye	1	#110, small	Plated
Wood filler	1 tube or small can		Matching wood color
Glue	1 small bottle		Woodworking
Sandpaper	2–3 sheets	100–150 grit	Medium and fine
Finish	1 can		Enamel or clear

Ark Assembly

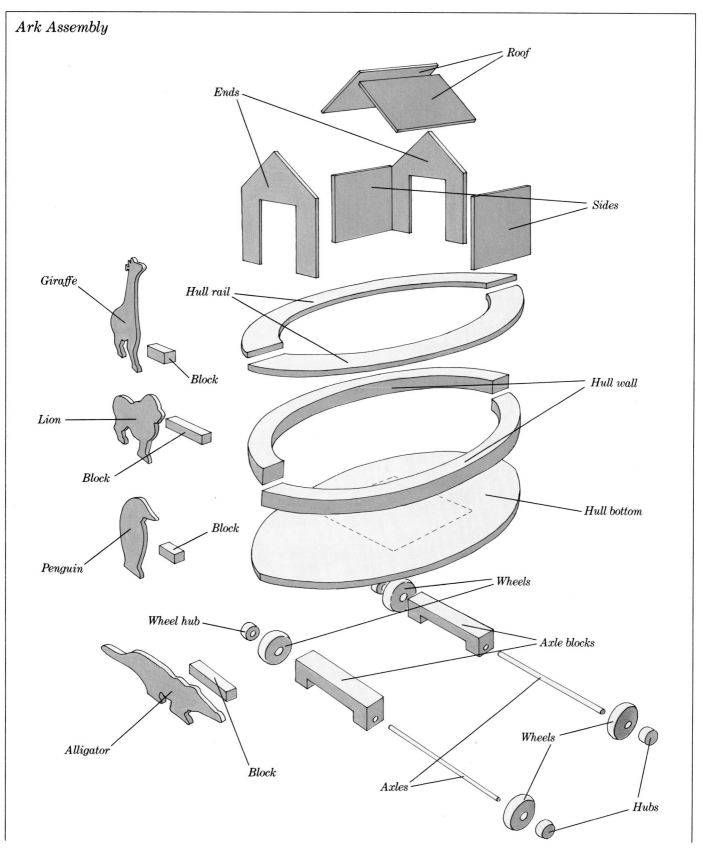

Roof

Ends

Sides

Giraffe

Hull rail

Block

Hull wall

Lion

Block

Hull bottom

Penguin

Block

Wheels

Wheel hub

Axle blocks

Alligator

Wheels

Block

Hubs

Axles

DUMPING PICKUP TRUCK

*T*his little truck is easy to build and makes a great gift. It will occupy one- to four-year-olds for hours.

This project can be built with hand tools only. However, it has a lot of square-cut, different-sized pieces. A table or radial arm saw with a smooth cutting blade would be very useful in making these cuts. If ¼-inch or ½-inch stock is not available, you will need a table saw or a band saw to rip that thickness. A drill with ¼-inch and ½-inch bits, a wood rasp, some C-clamps, and other ordinary hand tools are also needed. See the comments in Tools and Techniques on page 7.

Building Steps

1. Begin by cutting out the parts for the 1½-inch-thick motor housing and cab. If these parts are going to be made up from ¾-inch lumber, cut 2 pieces of each size specified. Face-glue the pairs together and clamp with C-clamps. Use pads under the clamps to spread the pressure and prevent marring.

2. While the glue is drying, continue to cut out the truck parts. Saw the base from the ¾-inch stock. Note from the illustrations that one end of the base is narrower than the other. These cuts can be made with a back-saw, a jigsaw, or a band saw.

3. Rip the ½-inch-square pieces for the front and back axle blocks in 2 passes from the 1 by 4 stock, and then cut them to length. When ripping, watch your fingers and use a push stick. The ½-inch-wide bed support is also simply ripped from the ¾-inch stock and cut to length.

4. The next sawing job is to cut the stock for the truck bed. It is all ¼ inch thick. Read Cutting Thin Stock on page 8. If you rip the stock yourself, take great care. Ripping pieces as thin as ¼ inch is tricky and can be dangerous if a power saw is used.

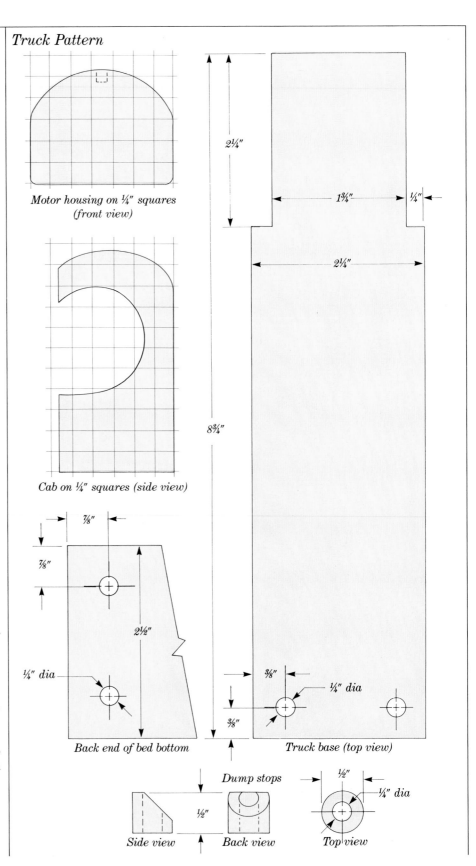

Truck Pattern

Motor housing on ¼" squares (front view)

Cab on ¼" squares (side view)

2¼"

1¾"   ¼"

2¼"

8¾"

⅞"

⅞"

2½"

¼" dia

Back end of bed bottom

⅜"

¼" dia

⅜"

Truck base (top view)

Dump stops

½"

Side view   Back view

½"

¼" dia

Top view

Materials List

Soft pine, such as ponderosa, white, or sugar pine, or a hardwood such as hard maple, birch, or cherry, are the woods of choice for this project.

Note that there are ¼-inch-, ½-inch-, ¾-inch-, and 1½-inch-thick pieces. You can make all these from 1-by stock by ripping it down to the ¼-inch and ½-inch thicknesses and gluing it up to the 1½-inch thickness. A piece of 1 by 4, approximately 6 feet long, is sufficient for making this truck. Cut all pieces out of clear sections of the lumber. The dowels should be hardwood.

Lumber

Piece	No. of Pieces	Thickness	Width	Length
Bed bottom	1	¼″	2½″	4¾″
Bed sides	2	¼″	¾″	4¾″
Bed ends	2	¼″	¾″	2″
Rear axle block	1	½″	½″	2¼″
Front axle block	1	½″	½″	1¾″
Bed support	1	½″	¾″	1½″
Base	1	¾″	2¼″	8¾″
Motor housing	1	1½″	1¾″	2¼″
Cab	1	1½″	2¼″	1⅞″
Radiator cap	1	¼″ dowel		½″
Hinges	2	¼″ dowel		1½″
Dump stops	2	½″ dowel		½″

Hardware and Miscellaneous

Item	Quantity	Size	Description
Wood wheels	4	1¾″ × ½″	With ¼″ axle holes
Axle pegs	4	¼″ × 1¼″	
Wire brads	8	½″	Finishing
Wood filler	1 tube or small can		Matching wood color
Glue	1 small bottle		Woodworking
Sandpaper	2 sheets	100–150 grit	Medium and fine
Finish	1 can		Enamel or clear

When the material is sized to ¼ inch, cut out the pieces for the bottom, sides, and ends of the truck bed.

5. Once the glue is dry, unclamp the motor housing and cab parts. These must be shaped. The motor housing has a flat bottom and a rounded top. (See the illustrations.) Shape it with a wood rasp or a stationary belt sander. (Watch your fingers!)

The cab shape is made with a curve-cutting saw such as a coping, band, or scroll saw, or a jigsaw. Smooth the curved cuts with your rasp when finished.

6. Now cut the radiator cap and the hinge pieces from a ¼-inch dowel. From a ½-inch dowel, cut a blank 4 inches long for the 2 dump stops.

7. Drill all the necessary holes. Check the illustration to locate them accurately. Start with a blind ¼-inch hole in the front of the motor housing for the radiator cap. This is about ½ inch deep.

Drill a ¼-inch hole through the center of the front and rear axle blocks. Be careful to keep them straight.

8. Drill a ¼-inch hole about ¾ inch deep through the center of both ends of the ½-inch dowel blank for the dump stops. After the holes are drilled, saw, rasp, or sand both ends of the dowel blank to a 45-degree angle. Cut a dump stop from each end. They are ½ inch long.

9. Carefully position the truck-bed bottom on top of the base, following the illustrations. Hold it in that temporary position with 1 or 2 clamps. Mark the position of the hinge dowels and drill down through both pieces, using a ¼-inch drill.

Your child will load up this handy truck and gleefully push it around. When the load needs dumping, the truck bed can be lifted up—and out comes the load.

Truck Assembly

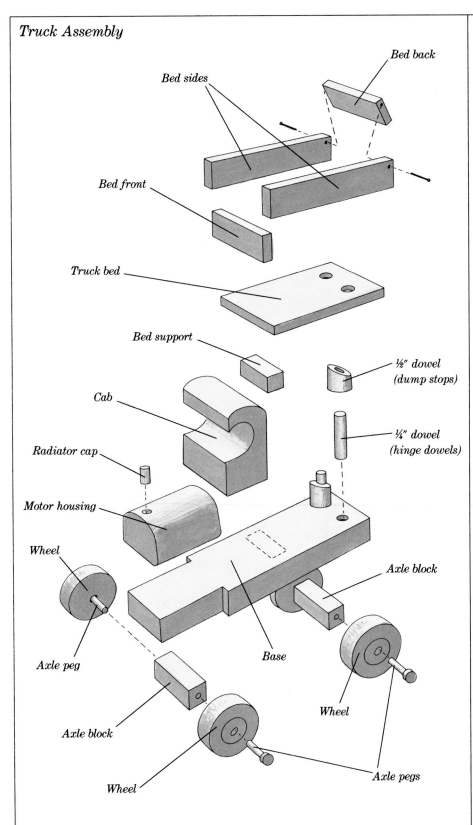

Bed back

Bed sides

Bed front

Truck bed

Bed support

½" dowel
(dump stops)

Cab

¼" dowel
(hinge dowels)

Radiator cap

Motor housing

Wheel

Axle block

Axle peg

Base

Wheel

Axle block

Axle pegs

Wheel

10. Give all the pieces a good once-over sanding, smoothing all surfaces. Be careful not to round edges or corners at this time. Set the pieces together and dry-fit to see if all the sizes are right.

11. Begin the final assembly by gluing the truck bed together. Use woodworking glue and the ½-inch brads. Clamp if necessary. With each gluing operation, wipe off any excess glue with a damp rag or sponge.

Next, position, glue, and clamp the 2 axle blocks on the bottom of the base. After the glue has set, glue the motor housing and cab to the base. Again, use clamps but be careful not to put too much pressure on the cab roof. It is cross-grained and could break. Glue the bed-support piece in position.

12. Apply a small amount of glue and tap the radiator cap into its hole, leaving about ¼ inch exposed. Insert and glue the 2 hinge dowels into their holes. Leave ¾ inch of the dowels exposed. When the glue has dried, round the ends of the hinge dowels with sandpaper. Slip the dump stops over the hinge dowels and glue in position.

13. Slip the bed assembly onto the hinge dowels to see if it fits. You are going to have to widen the 2 holes in the bed so that the bed will tilt to about 45 degrees. Use a ¼-inch drill or rat-tail file for this.

14. Now do the final sanding. Sand off any saw or machining marks, round all the corners and edges, and smooth all the surfaces. Fill any cracks or holes and sand them smooth.

15. Finally, put the wheels onto the axle pegs, apply a little glue onto the ends of the pegs, and tap them into the holes in the axle blocks.

16. If you used an attractive wood, you may elect to use a clear finish such as varnish, lacquer, or wax for the truck. Otherwise, paint it the color of your choice. Spray paint is recommended as it is easily applied, dries quickly, and is easy to clean up. Be sure to read the instructions on the can and use in a well-ventilated location. Apply at least 2 coats of finish.

BOBBING TURTLE

The head and tail of this landlubber turtle bob up and down as your one- to four-year-old pulls it across the floor. The project is a sandwich of wood pieces that shape the outer body but conceal the wheels and the small cam mechanism that causes the action.

Most of the cuts for this bobbing turtle are curved. A power jigsaw, scroll saw, or band saw with a narrow blade will facilitate these cuts, although you can use a hand coping saw. You also need a drill with ⅛-inch, ⁹⁄₆₄-inch, and ¹⁷⁄₆₄-inch bits and other ordinary hand tools. Several clamps with 5-inch openings are required for the assembly. See the comments in Tools and Techniques on page 7.

Building Steps

1. Start this project by cutting out 5 body pieces. First, saw the blanks for these pieces; they should be 2½ inches by 6 inches. Since all have the same outside shape, it will be easier to stack 2 or more pieces and gang-saw them. See Duplicate Sawing or Drilling on page 9 for tips on how to join stacked pieces temporarily. The size of the stack you can cut will depend on the type of saw you are using. After tracing the pattern on the stack or stacks, saw with a coping saw, jigsaw, scroll saw, or band saw. Leave one pair of body pieces stacked together.

2. The stacked pair will be the inner body pieces. Copy the pattern for the wheel housing to the joined pieces, and saw them out. A hand coping saw or power scroll saw is the preferred tool for this cut, since the radius is small. If you are making the cuts with a jigsaw or band saw, use a very narrow blade. Separate the 2 pieces when you are done.

3. Draw the outline of the center body piece and saw it to shape.

4. Make the turtle head-and-tail piece: Draw the side pattern on a 9-inch-long piece of ¾-inch stock and saw it out carefully. Again, a coping or scroll saw works best here.

5. Locate the pivot hole from the illustrations and drill a ⁹⁄₆₄-inch hole through the head-and-tail piece.

Draw the top pattern and saw it, leaving the head ¾ inch wide and the body and tail ½ inch wide. Using a rasp or belt sander, carefully shape the head and tail ends. Finish this piece with a good sanding.

6. There are still 2 turtle body pieces with no cuts or shapes on the underside. These are the outer body pieces. Identify and mark the inside and outside of each piece, choosing the best face for the outside. From the illustrations locate the position of the axle holes and mark these on the insides of the pieces. Using a stop on the drill or drill press, bore the two ¹⁷⁄₆₄-inch axle holes, ⅜ inch deep. Be

Most turtles move slowly, but this one will keep up with the fastest youngster. The head and tail bob up and down as it is pulled along.

Bobbing Turtle Assembly

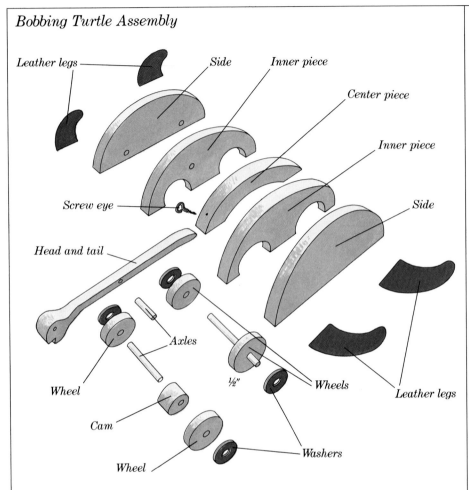

Leather legs — Side — Inner piece — Center piece — Inner piece — Screw eye — Side — Head and tail — Axles — Wheel — ½" — Wheels — Cam — Leather legs — Wheel — Washers

careful with the depth—you don't want to go all the way through.

7. Now get the 2 inner body pieces with the wheel cutouts. Locate the pivot holes (see the illustration). Using a ⅛-inch drill bit, drill these holes into the insides of the pieces. Make them ⅜ inch deep. As you did with the axle holes, use a depth stop.

8. Study the cam design in the illustrations. Copy the cam shape onto a small piece of ¾-inch stock. Locate and drill the ¼-inch hole. Using a fine-tooth saw, cut out the shape of the cam. Smooth and round the cam with a rasp or sandpaper or both.

9. Now cut two 4-inch lengths from a piece of ¼-inch hardwood dowel. These are the axle dowels. Lightly sand them, removing burrs and fuzz.

Apply glue to the center of one of the axles and slide the cam onto it, centering it carefully.

10. Carefully note the location of the wheels on the axles from the illustration, and mark their places. Apply glue to the axles and slide the wheels into place.

11. The last piece to be cut is the ⅛-inch pivot dowel. Cut it 1½ inches long. Sand it lightly.

12. Look over the illustrations and the pictures carefully to see how everything fits together. Note the location of the washers on each side of head-and-tail piece. Wax the ends of the axles and the axle holes in the body sides before assembly.

Lay one outer body piece flat on its side on a table or workbench. Put one of the inner body sides on top of it. Insert the front and back axle-wheel assemblies. Insert the ⅛-inch

dowel, a washer, the head-and-tail piece, and another washer. Then add the center body piece, the second inner body piece, and finally the second outer piece. Holding it firmly in your hand, clamp the assembly together. Don't forget to use pads between the turtle body and the clamps to prevent marring. Label all of the body pieces for position.

Now try it out. Make sure the wheels turn freely and the head-and-tail assembly moves easily without hitting anything.

13. Sand to remove saw marks and to smooth the edges of the sandwiched pieces. Remove the wheel assemblies and the head-and-tail piece. Reclamp the body pieces together in their correct position, and sand the bottom and the curved top flush. A stationary belt sander would work best for this, if one is available. Otherwise, use a wood rasp and hand-sanding equipment.

14. Start the final assembly. Follow step 12 again, except this time use glue between the pieces. Be careful not to get any glue in or near the axle or pivot holes. Clamp, and wipe off any excess glue. Before the glue sets, check all the pieces to make sure everything turns and moves freely.

15. When the glue has set, shape the outside edges of the turtle to give it a rounded shape. Fill any defects or holes with wood filler. When dry, give the entire toy a final sanding.

16. Use several coats of finish. If you like the appearance of the wood, use a wax or clear lacquer or varnish finish. Otherwise, use a bright enamel paint. Be careful not to let the finish get into the working parts of the turtle and cause them to stick.

17. Consult the illustration for the leg shapes. Draw the patterns on pieces of scrap leather or vinyl, and cut them out. Using the ½-inch brads, tack them onto the bottom of the turtle as show in the illustrations.

18. Finally, screw the screw eye into the front center of the turtle. Attach the pull cord.

Turtle Pattern on ½″ Squares

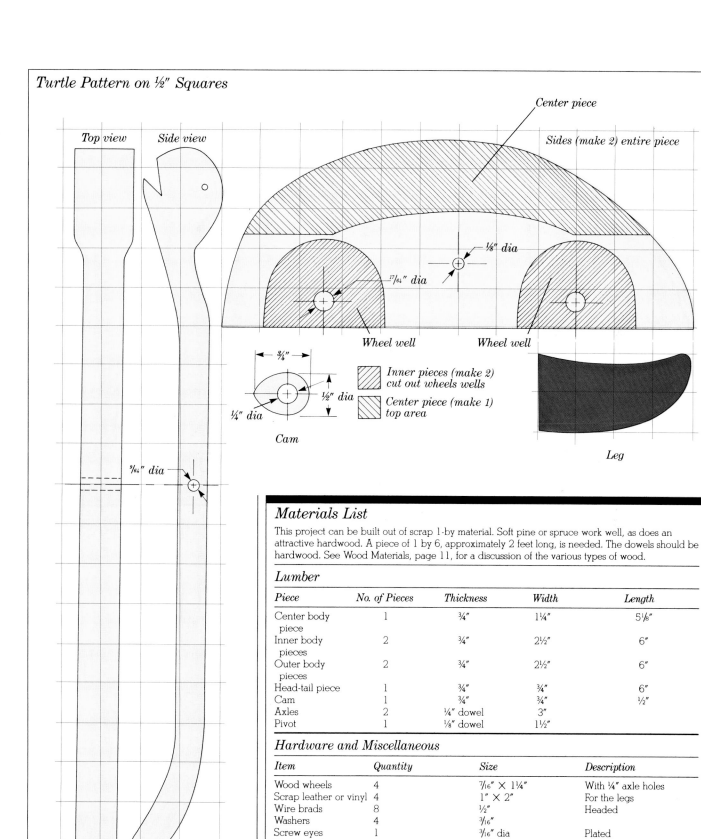

Top view Side view

Center piece

Sides (make 2) entire piece

⅛″ dia

¹⁷/₆₄″ dia

Wheel well   Wheel well

¾″

¼″ dia   ½″ dia

Cam

Inner pieces (make 2) cut out wheels wells

Center piece (make 1) top area

Leg

⁹/₆₄″ dia

Materials List

This project can be built out of scrap 1-by material. Soft pine or spruce work well, as does an attractive hardwood. A piece of 1 by 6, approximately 2 feet long, is needed. The dowels should be hardwood. See Wood Materials, page 11, for a discussion of the various types of wood.

Lumber

Piece	No. of Pieces	Thickness	Width	Length
Center body piece	1	¾″	1¼″	5⅛″
Inner body pieces	2	¾″	2½″	6″
Outer body pieces	2	¾″	2½″	6″
Head-tail piece	1	¾″	¾″	6″
Cam	1	¾″	¾″	½″
Axles	2	¼″ dowel		3″
Pivot	1	⅛″ dowel		1½″

Hardware and Miscellaneous

Item	Quantity	Size	Description
Wood wheels	4	⁷/₁₆″ × 1¼″	With ¼″ axle holes
Scrap leather or vinyl	4	1″ × 2″	For the legs
Wire brads	8	½″	Headed
Washers	4	³/₁₆″	
Screw eyes	1	³/₁₆″ dia	Plated
Plastic cord	1	36″	
Wood filler	1 tube or small can		Matching wood color
Glue	1 small bottle		Woodworking
Sandpaper	2 sheets	100–150 grit	Medium and fine
Finish	1 small can		Enamel or clear

FARM TRACTOR

T *his toy replica of the old farm tractor is certain to delight children of all ages, but especially those from one to five.*

The tractor can be made with common hand tools, including a coping saw, a wood rasp, and a drill with ⅛-inch, ³⁄₁₆-inch, and ⅜-inch bits.

If available, a jigsaw, scroll saw, or band saw with a narrow blade, and a drill press would be useful. See the comments in Tools and Techniques on page 7.

Building Steps

1. If you are using ¾-inch-thick material, begin by face-gluing sufficient material to cut the tractor body and fenders. Glue and clamp, using pads between the clamps and the piece to spread the pressure and prevent marring.

2. Draw the tractor-body pattern on 1½-inch stock. See Transferring Shapes From Illustrations on page 13. Cut the outside shape, both side and top, using a hand coping saw or a scroll saw. If you have one, you can also use a jigsaw or band saw equipped with a narrow blade.

3. Drill a ⅜-inch entrance hole for the saw blade in the engine-compartment opening. Detach the saw blade from the coping or scroll saw, insert it through the hole, reattach the blade, and carefully saw out the inside area. A jigsaw can also be used for this cut.

4. Draw the 2 fender shapes on the 1½-inch stock and saw out.

5. Saw the engine block from a piece of scrap.

6. There are a number of holes to drill. Since you need to position them accurately, brad-pointed bits are helpful.

Start with the two ³⁄₁₆-inch axle holes. Use the illustration to locate these and drill them out. To prevent the drill bit from splitting the wood

Tractor Pattern on ¼″ Squares

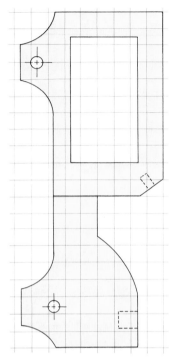

Tractor body (side view)

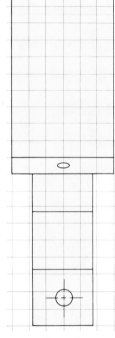

Tractor body (top view)

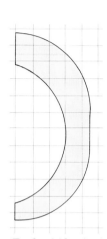

Fender (side view)

All this Farm Tractor needs is a miniature field of corn to plow. But crayons and a little imagination work just as well.

Tractor Assembly

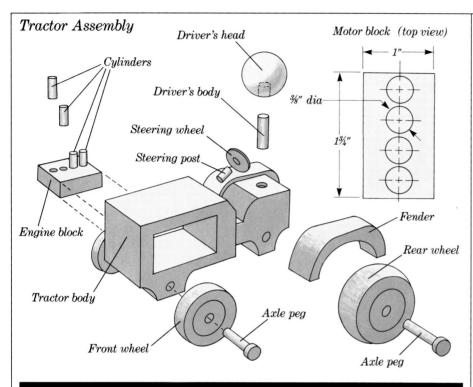

Cylinders, **Driver's head**, **Driver's body**, **Steering wheel**, **Steering post**, **Engine block**, **Tractor body**, **Front wheel**, **Axle peg**, **Fender**, **Rear wheel**, **Axle peg**

Motor block *(top view)*
1″, ⅜″ dia, 1¾″

Materials List

This project is made from a small scrap piece of 1½-inch-thick wood such as a 2 by 4 end. Softwood, such as spruce, ponderosa pine, or white pine, or a hardwood such as hard maple, birch, or cherry, will all work for this project. If the 1½-inch-thick stock is not handy, you can face-glue ¾-inch wood. Cut all pieces out of clear sections of the lumber. The short dowel pieces are hardwood. See Wood Materials on page 11.

Lumber

Piece	No. of Pieces	Thickness	Width	Length
Engine block	1	½″	1″	1¾″
Tractor body	1	1½″	2¼″	5″
Fenders	2	1½″	3½″	3″
Driver body	1	⅛″ dowel	1″	
Steering-wheel post	1	⅛″ dowel	1″	
Cylinders	⅜″ dowel	¾″		

Hardware and Miscellaneous

Item	Quantity	Size	Description
Wood wheel	1	¼″ × ¾″	With ⅛″ axle hole
Wood wheels	2	⅜″ × 1¼″	With 3/16″ axle holes
Wood wheels	2	⅝″ × 2″	With 3/16″ axle holes
Axle pegs	4	3/16″ × 1¼″	
Wood ball	1	1″ dia	Driver's head
Glue	1 small bottle		Woodworking
Sandpaper	2 sheets	100–150 grit	Medium and fine
Finish	1 can		Enamel or clear

when it emerges, use a piece of scrap wood for backup. Use a drill press if you have one: They must be drilled square and straight.

Drill the four ⅜-inch cylinder holes in the motor block. These go completely through the piece. Again, these need to be square and straight. Drill a ⅛-inch blind hole, about ¾ inch deep, in the seat area for the driver-body dowel. Drill another in the tractor dash area for the steering-wheel post. Check the illustration for the correct locations and angles.

Drill a ⅛-inch blind hole into the center of the 1-inch wood ball (the driver's head).

7. From a ⅛-inch dowel, cut the driver body and steering-wheel post. Cut the 4 cylinder pieces from a ⅜-inch dowel.

8. Sand the shapes smooth. You may need to use a wood rasp before sanding. Progress from medium- to fine-grit paper.

9. Set all the pieces up on a workbench and check to see if everything fits. If all is well, start the assembly by inserting and gluing the cylinders in the motor block. Take care here—if the cylinders fit too tightly they could split the block when driven home. If necessary, sand the cylinder dowels until they fit snugly but not tightly. Apply glue and tap into place. Wipe off any excess glue with a damp rag.

10. Now glue the motor assembly inside the tractor-body motor housing. This will be difficult to clamp. Use a light coating of glue on both surfaces, and hold it for a minute or so with your fingers until the glue starts to set.

11. Glue and clamp the fenders to the body sides. Use scrap blocks on the outside of the fenders to spread the clamp pressure and prevent marring.

12. Glue and tap the steering-wheel post and the driver-body dowel into place. Use the glue sparingly. Read Gluing Dowels on page 11 before doing this. Take care to not set these 2 dowels too deep.

13. Glue the driver-head ball on the end of the body dowel and glue the steering wheel on the end of the steering-wheel post. Wipe off excess glue when necessary.

14. Insert the axle pegs through the wheels, apply glue to the end, and tap into the axle holes.

15. All that remains is a final sanding and finish. Spray paint is simple and easy. Use spray enamel or a clear varnish or lacquer, depending upon the wood used and your preference. Follow the directions on the can carefully, and apply 2 or 3 coats. A wax finish is another option for this toy.

CIRCUS TRAIN

Reminiscent of old Barnum and Bailey trains, this locomotive and cage cars can carry any cargo your three- to five-year-old wishes to haul. This project is approximately 16 inches long when finished, but you can add as many cars as you want to make it longer.

Although this toy can be built entirely with hand tools, several power tools will facilitate construction. The project has a number of square-cut, different-sized pieces. A table or radial arm saw with a smooth cutting blade would be very useful in making these cuts. A drill press would be especially useful for drilling the dowel holes in the cars, as would a belt sander for flushing and shaping the parts.

You need a coping saw, jigsaw, or scroll saw to make the curved inside cuts. Other tool requirements include ⅛-inch, ¼-inch, and ½-inch drill bits; a wood rasp; some C-clamps; and ordinary hand tools. See the comments in Tools and Techniques on page 7.

Building Steps

1. Begin by sawing all the pieces of the cage cars to the specified dimensions. This includes the 3 cage-car bases, the cage rims, the cage tops, and the cage-top centering blocks. Cut all of these from the ¼-inch plywood. Rip the 6 cage-car axle blocks from ¾-inch stock. Use a radial arm or table saw for this job, if one is available. Use a plywood-cutting or a fine-tooth cabinet saw blade to minimize edge splintering.

2. The next step is to drill all the holes for the dowel bars. At first glance this may seem like quite a chore. However, if you stack and temporarily join all the base and rim pieces, you can drill all the holes at once. See Duplicate Sawing or Drilling on page 9 for ideas on how to join the pieces temporarily. Use a drill press to bore these holes. They must be square and straight. Mark the 20 hole locations on the piece on top, using a tracing from the illustrations. See Transferring Shapes From Illustrations on page 13. With an awl, prick or indent the center of each hole to keep the drill bit from skating. Use a piece of scrap wood under the stack to keep the drill bit from splitting the wood when it emerges. Drill each hole with a ⅛-inch drill bit, using a relatively high speed to get the cleanest hole possible.

3. Drill the axle-peg holes in the axle blocks. Note their location from the illustrations. The hole size is ⅛ inch in diameter; drill all the way through the block. Take care that all

This train can be made with as many cars as you wish. The tops of the cars lift off to allow easy loading and unloading before the train chugs to the next stop.

holes are straight and square with the ends of the blocks.

4. Now go back to the stacked base and rim pieces. Separate 3 of the pieces from the stack. These will be the car bases. The 3 remaining will be the cage rims. Note from the illustrations that the center parts of the rim pieces are cut out, making them, in effect, hollow rectangles. Draw the inside cutout lines on the top of the stack.

Drill a saw-blade entrance hole inside the cutout. Using a coping saw, jigsaw, or scroll saw, cut this inside rectangle out. Saw slowly and carefully to save future sanding.

5. Cut the ⅛-inch cage-bar dowels. Since there are 60 of these and they must be cut evenly, you will want to rig up a stop or some other arrangement to cut these dowels to the same length easily and safely. If you are using a table saw, you can use the stop rods on the miter gauge. You can also clamp a stop block on the fence on either a table or radial arm saw. Or you can drill a blind ⁵⁄₃₂-inch hole the correct depth (1⅜ inches) in a small block. Then use the block to hold the short dowel while sawing.

Note that sawing small, short dowels with a power saw is tricky and can be dangerous. Use the finest-tooth blade possible. It will help keep the

blade from snagging the small dowel. With a table saw, keep the blade as low as possible. Don't set up so that the cut dowel piece can get trapped between the fence and the turning blade. Take special care; your fingers get very close to the revolving saw blade here. If you have any doubts, saw the dowels by hand.

6. After the cage bars are all cut to length, give them a light sanding, using fine-grit sandpaper. Give the edges and flat surfaces of all the other pieces a good sanding to remove saw marks and fuzz and to smooth the surfaces. Progress from medium-grit to fine-grit sandpaper. Don't round any edges or corners at this time; do this after assembly.

7. Start the assembly by applying glue and tapping the bar dowels into one of the car bases. Drive the dowels down until they are just flush with the bottom of the base. Use glue very sparingly, and be careful not to burr or damage the tops of the dowels. Check to be sure that the installed bar dowels are all straight and evenly spaced. Apply a small amount of glue to the top of each dowel. Carefully align the cage rim, and press down on the dowels. Tap the rim down until the dowels are flush with the top surface. Use a block between the hammer and the rim piece to avoid marring the surface. As soon as you are done, wipe off any excess glue with a damp rag or sponge.

Set this first cage car aside to allow the glue to set, and assemble the other 2 cars.

8. After all the cars are thoroughly dry, sand the tops of the cage rims and the bottoms of the bases so that the dowel ends are smooth and flush. Use a stationary belt sander for this if you have one. Otherwise, put a sheet of sandpaper flat on the workbench and sand by moving the cage back and forth on the paper. If needed, fill any cracks or holes with wood filler. Sand flush when dry.

9. Attach the axle blocks by gluing them in place. Locate the position from the illustrations. Clamp with C-clamps until the glue has set. Use

Circus Train Pattern

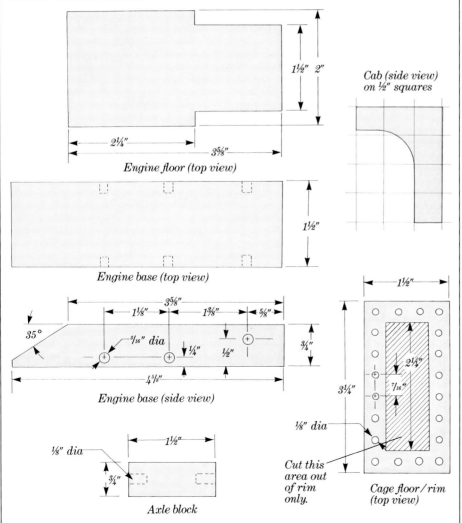

Engine floor (top view)

Engine base (top view)

Engine base (side view)

Axle block

Cab (side view) on ½" squares

Cut this area out of rim only.

Cage floor/rim (top view)

Engine Assembly

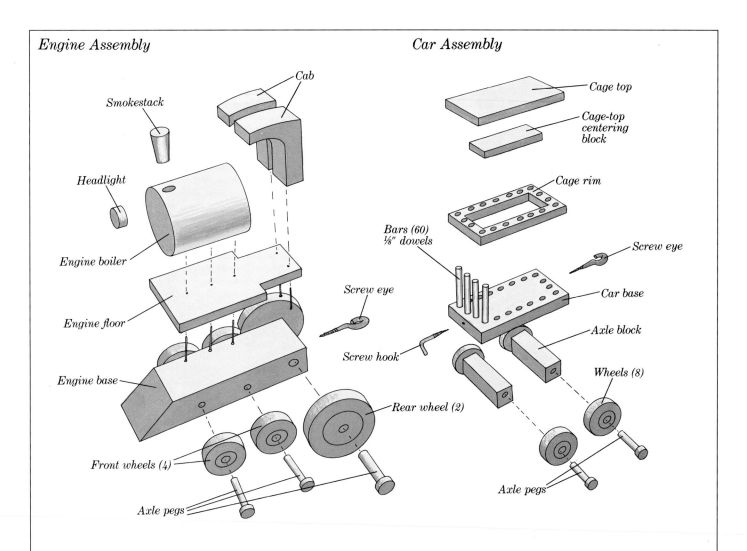

Smokestack

Cab

Headlight

Engine boiler

Engine floor

Engine base

Front wheels (4)

Axle pegs

Screw eye

Screw hook

Rear wheel (2)

Car Assembly

Cage top

Cage-top centering block

Cage rim

Bars (60) ⅛" dowels

Screw eye

Car base

Axle block

Wheels (8)

Axle pegs

small scraps of wood as pads under the clamp jaws to prevent marring.

10. While the glue is drying, assemble the cage-car tops and centering blocks. Position the centering blocks on the undersides of the tops, and glue them in place. Use clamps to ensure a good glue bond. If you have run out of clamps, you can use some very small brads, less than ½ inch long. Wipe off any excess glue.

11. Give the 3 cars a final sanding, this time rounding all the edges and corners.

12. Attach the wheels. Slip the 1-inch-diameter turned wheels onto the ends of the ⅛-inch axle pegs, apply a small amount of glue, and tap the pegs into the holes in the axle block.

Take care not to drive them too tight, or the wheels won't turn. The hooking hardware is added after the cars are finished.

13. Saw out the blanks for the engine base and the 2 pieces for the engine cab from ¾-inch stock. Cut the engine floor from ¼-inch plywood. Face-glue the 2 engine cab pieces to make one piece, 1½ inches thick. Carefully align them so that the edges are flush, and draw them together with C-clamps. Again, use pads between the clamps and the piece to avoid marring.

14. Make the angle cut on the front of the engine base for the cowcatcher. If you are using a table or radial arm saw, set the miter gauge or saw to make a 30-degree cut.

15. Saw the notches out of the sides of the engine floor. Use a coping saw, jigsaw, or band saw for these cuts.

16. After the glue is dry, remove the clamps from the engine cab piece and draw the curved shape shown in the illustrations. Saw this out, using a coping or scroll saw or a jigsaw or band saw with a narrow blade. Smooth the inside curve with the round side of a wood rasp.

17. Cut a 2-inch length of 1½-inch dowel for the engine boiler. Flatten the bottom as shown in the illustration so that the boiler will lie flat on the engine floor. You can do this with a stationary belt sander or with a plane or wood rasp. If you flatten it by hand, smooth the flattened side by rubbing it back and forth on a piece of sandpaper held flat on a workbench.

18. Now mark the various hole locations shown in the illustrations. This includes the two ⅛-inch axle holes and the one 3/16-inch axle hole in the engine base. The ½-inch blind hole for the headlight and the ¼-inch blind hole for the smokestack are located on the engine boiler. Both of these holes are ½ inch deep. Drill all of these holes, taking care to keep them square and straight.

19. Cut the two ½-inch dowels for the headlight and smokestack. Using a sharp knife and sandpaper, shape the smokestack dowel to the tapered shape shown in the illustrations. One end of the dowel should be tapered to slightly less than ¼ inch in diameter. Apply glue and tap both pieces into their respective holes. The smokestack should protrude about ⅜ inch and the headlight ¼ inch.

20. Sand all the engine parts. Begin with medium-grit and finish with fine-grit sandpaper.

21. To assemble the engine, first study the illustrations for the correct position of the parts. Start by attaching the cab and boiler to the engine floor. Use glue and the ¾-inch brads to strengthen the joints. Take care when driving the brads up into the bottom of the cab. The cross grain in the cab roof could break if the piece is not held squarely.

Materials List

The main components of this project are cut from ¼-inch Baltic birch plywood; several pieces of ¾-inch solid wood, either pine or hardwood; and hardwood dowels. You will need a piece of plywood about 1 foot square and approximately 8 lineal feet of ⅛-inch dowel stock. For more information on choosing woods, see Wood Materials, page 11.

Lumber

Piece	No. of Pieces	Thickness	Width	Length
Cage-car bases	3	¼" plywood	1½"	3¼"
Cage rims	3	¼" plywood	1½"	3¼"
Cage tops	3	¼" plywood	1½"	3¼"
Cage-top centering blocks	3	¼" plywood	¾"	2⅜"
Engine floor	1	¼" plywood	2"	3⅝"
Axle blocks	6	½"	¾"	1½"
Engine base	1	¾"	1½"	4½"
Engine cab	2	¾"	1½"	2"
Cage bars	60	⅛" dowel	1⅜"	
Light and smokestack	2	½" dowel	¾"	
Engine boiler	1	1½" dowel	2"	

Hardware and Miscellaneous

Item	Quantity	Size	Description
Wood wheels	16	¼" × 1"	With ⅛" axle holes
Wood wheels	2	⅜" × 1½"	With 3/16" axle holes
Axle pegs	2	3/16" × 1⅜"	Turned hardwood
Axle pegs	16	⅛" × ⅞"	Turned hardwood
Wire brads	6	¾"	Finishing
Screw eyes	4	Small	Plated
Screw hooks	3	Small	Plated
Wood filler	1 tube or small can		Matching wood color
Glue	1 small bottle		Woodworking
Sandpaper	2–3 sheets	100–150 grit	Medium and fine
Finish	1 can		Enamel or clear

22. Glue and clamp the engine-floor assembly to the engine base. Locate the clamps carefully so that no damage is done to the boiler or cab.

23. Finally, attach the wheels. Slip the front four 1-inch-diameter turned wheels onto the ends of the ⅛-inch axle pegs, apply a small amount of glue, and tap the pegs into the axle holes in the engine base. The 2 rear 1½-inch wheels fit on the larger 3/16-inch axle pegs. Again, take care not to drive them too tightly or the wheels will not turn.

24. Before putting a finish on the project, give the engine and the cage cars a final light sanding and then blow off all dust.

You may elect to use a clear finish showing the attractive wood grain or to use a bright, glossy enamel paint.

If you use spray paint, be sure to use it in a well-ventilated location. However you apply the clear finish or paint, be careful not to get too much on the wheels and axle pegs or they will not turn. Give each wheel a turn before the finish has set tight.

25. Attach the screw eyes in the backs of the engine and the first 2 cars and the screw hooks in the fronts of the cars. Refer to the illustrations for the correct locations.

LITTLE RED WAGON

I *magine the sparkle in your two- to six-year-old's eyes when you present him or her with this little wagon. Lots of toys, as well as a few select friends, will get free rides. When it isn't loaded, it can serve as a seat.*

You need a table or radial arm saw to make this project. The straight, square cuts ensure a good fit, and you will need to rip the ½-inch side pieces and cut the rabbet joints. A jigsaw or band saw will help in cutting out the wheels, yoke, and axle supports. Other tools you need include basic hand tools: a drill with ½-inch and 9/16-inch bits and bar and C-clamps for the assembly. See the comments in Tools and Techniques on page 7.

Building Steps

1. Cut out the wagon box pieces: Cut the bottom from the ½-inch birch plywood, making sure it is perfectly square. Saw the 2 end pieces and the 2 side pieces from the ¾-inch solid wood stock. Before cutting the final length of the end pieces, read the note at the end of step 2.

2. Machine the 2 side pieces down to ½-inch thickness. Review Cutting Thin Stock on page 8. As that section describes, you have several options. One is to surface the pieces to ½-inch thickness with a planer. Another is to rip the pieces on edge with a band or table saw, using a smooth-cut rip blade, and then jointing, planing, or sanding to smooth the sawn face. If you do the resizing on the table saw, take special care. Use a push stick and watch your fingers.

Note: Reducing the thickness of the sides keeps the wagon weight down and looks good. However, if you

desire, you can leave the sides at their original ¾-inch thickness. In that case the end pieces should be cut 11½ inches long.

3. Cut rabbets on the ends and inside bottom edge of each end piece to make rabbeted butt joints with the ½-inch-thick bottom and side pieces. The dimensions for the rabbet are ½ inch wide by ½ inch deep. Also cut rabbets, ¼-inch deep by ½-inch wide, along the inside bottom edge of the side pieces. If available, use a dado blade for making the rabbets. Otherwise, you can cut them with 2 passes of the saw. Another alternative is to cut the rabbets with

a router and ½-inch rabbeting bit. Note: If you left the sides at their original ¾-inch thickness, the rabbet dimensions should be ½ inch deep by ¾ inch wide.

4. Assemble the wagon box pieces. First, set all the pieces up on a workbench and check for fit. If everything appears to fit, give the pieces a good sanding. Use a hand or stationary power sander, if available. Start with medium-grit sandpaper, then move to fine-grit paper. Be careful not to round the end edges and corners of all the pieces at this time.

5. Now proceed by assembling the wagon frame (ends and sides) using

Whether it's hauling children or carting loads of important toy cargo, this wagon is bound to be full most of the time.

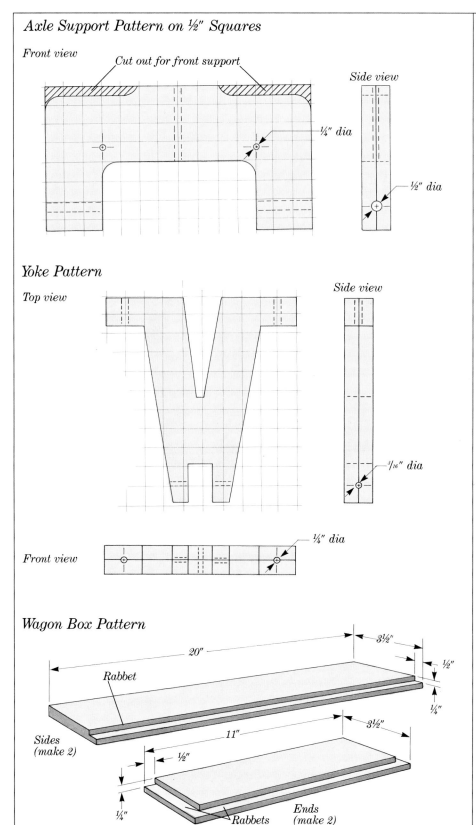

Axle Support Pattern on ½" Squares

Front view

Cut out for front support

¼" dia

Side view

½" dia

Yoke Pattern

Top view

Side view

³/₁₆" dia

Front view

¼" dia

Wagon Box Pattern

20"

3½"

½"

¼"

Rabbet

Sides
(make 2)

11"

3½"

½"

¼"

Rabbets

Ends
(make 2)

glue and 1¼-inch nails. Clamp in both directions, using bar or pipe clamps and taking care to use clamp pads to prevent marring. After the glue has dried, remove the clamps. Insert the bottom into the frame rabbets. Glue and nail in place using 1-inch nails. For both gluing steps, carefully wipe off any excess glue with a damp rag or sponge.

Drill a ¼-inch hole for the pivot bolt through the bottom of the wagon box. Refer to the illustrations for the hole location. Use a piece of scrap underneath the bottom to keep the drill from tearing the grain as it emerges.

6. While the box is drying, start on the wagon wheels. Study the illustrations carefully. You will see that each wheel is made of 2 pieces of ¾-inch stock, glue-laminated together. The 6-inch-diameter inner wheel is solid; the outer rim is a 6-inch circle with a 4-inch diameter circle cut out of it. Glued together, the wheel assembly is 1½ inches thick.

From the ¾-inch stock, cut all eight 6½-inch-square blanks for the wheels and outer wheel rims. Draw corner-to-corner diagonal lines on each piece to locate the center, and then draw a 6-inch-diameter circle with a drawing compass.

Starting with 4 of the blanks for the inner wheels, saw the 6-inch outside circles using a band saw or a hand-held jigsaw or saber saw. You can also use a coping or scroll saw. Use a narrow, fine-tooth blade. Depending upon the type of saw you are using, you may want to gang-saw the circles to save time and effort. See Duplicate Sawing or Drilling on page 9 for more details on gang-sawing curves.

Note: You can saw the circles, guiding by hand, and then sand them smooth. However, there are many techniques for jigging to saw round circles. Consult your woodworking reference books for this. Of course, you could also turn the wheels on a lathe for a true and smooth circle. In that case, you should face-glue the wheel and outer-wheel rim pieces first and turn them together.

7. Next, make the outer rims from the remaining 4 blanks. Start by sawing out the inner 4-inch circles: With the compass draw the circles using the previously marked centers. Drill a hole inside of the line for the saw blade, and cut the inside circles using a jigsaw, coping saw, or scroll saw. Saw slowly and carefully to save future sanding. Stack the blanks and gang-saw if appropriate.

Finally, saw the outside 6-inch circles. In addition to the other saws mentioned, a band saw can be used for this outside cut.

8. Before gluing the 2 wheel pieces together, sand the inside edges of the outer-wheel rims smooth. A drum sander works well for this. However you do this sanding, be careful not to turn or round the inside edges.

9. Align the edges, and nail and glue the rim to the wheel. Use the

1¼-inch nails. Check the illustrations for details. Clamp with C-clamps.

10. While the glue is drying, cut the axles to length. You can use steel pipe, rod, or hardwood dowels. The outside diameter must be ½ inch. Next, drill a ½-inch test hole in a piece of scrap and try inserting the axles in this hole. You want a close, but not tight, fit. If it is too tight, try out your next larger drill bit (¹⁷/₃₂ inch or ⁹/₁₆ inch), or slightly enlarge the hole with a rat-tail file. After determining the correct hole size, drill this hole in the center of each wheel assembly.

11. Countersink the nails and fill the holes with wood filler. When dry, sand the wheels smooth. If you have a disk or belt sander, a good way to smooth the outside edge is to insert an axle in the wheel hole and, holding it firmly, rotate the wheel against the moving sander.

Round the inner and outer edges of the wheel. A router with a ⅛-inch or ¼-inch round-over bit works well for this, as does a flap sander.

12. Next, go back to the table saw and cut out the blanks for the 2 axle supports. If ¾-inch stock is used, you need 4 pieces. They must be face-glued to make up the 1½-inch thickness. Finally, draw the cutouts or pockets (see illustrations) and saw them out using a jigsaw, coping, scroll, or band saw with a narrow blade.

13. Drill the ½-inch axle holes through the 2 stub ends of each axle support. These holes need to be square and aligned. The drill bit will probably not go all the way through both stubs, so you must mark the hole locations carefully and drill from each end. Use a drill press for this, if possible. Check to make sure the axles fit all the way through. Use a rat-tail file if needed to slightly alter the hole size or alignment. Finally, drill a ¼-inch hole through the center of the top edge of the front axle support for the ¼-inch pivot bolt.

14. Give the axle supports a good sanding to remove the saw marks on the edges and smooth all surfaces. You might want to round all the edges (except the top edges) using a router with a round-over bit or a flap sander.

15. The yoke is made of 2 pieces of the ½-inch plywood laminated together to provide the needed strength. Cut out two 5-inch squares for the blanks, and face-glue, clamping with C-clamps. Be sure to pad the clamps to prevent marring. After

Wagon Assembly

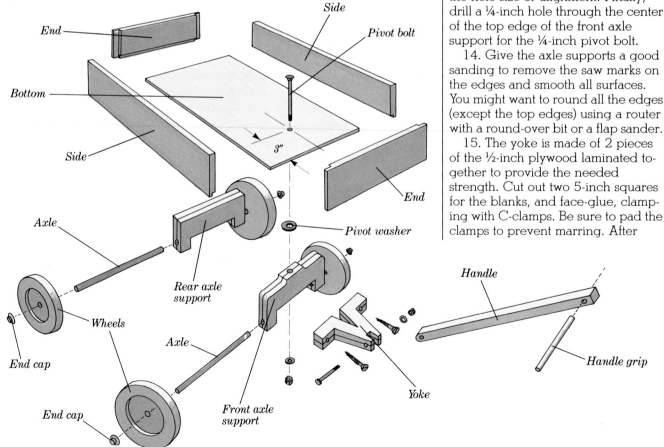

glue has set, remove the clamps and draw the yoke pattern from the illustrations. Cut out with a jigsaw, coping, scroll, or band saw.

16. Mark and drill the ³/₁₆-inch hole through the yoke tangs for the handle bolt, following the illustrations. On both ends of the hole, drill a shallow ¼-inch indentation hole to recess the bolt head and nut. Again, check the illustrations for details. Do this carefully to ensure centering and to prevent the grain from tearing. Finally, give the yoke a good sanding to remove saw marks, smooth the surfaces, and round the edges.

17. Rip the handle from the ¾-inch stock. Drill a ⅜-inch hole in one end for the dowel grip and a ³/₁₆-inch hole for bolting the handle to the yoke. Use a backup scrap to keep the drill from tearing the grain. Finally, sand the piece.

18. Cut the ⅜-inch dowel to length for the handle grip; sand both ends round. Apply glue to the center of the dowel and insert it into the handle, centering it carefully.

19. Countersink all the nails in the assembled wagon box, and fill the holes with wood filler. When dry, thoroughly sand the box, rounding all the edges. Be sure to sand off any traces of excess glue.

20. Start the final assembly by positioning the yoke on the front axle support, clamping it if necessary, and drilling 2 pilot screw holes through the yoke tabs into the support. Check the illustration for their location. Countersink these holes. Apply glue and screw the yoke into place.

21. Position and clamp the rear axle support on the bottom of the wagon box. Again, drill 2 or 3 countersunk pilot screw holes down through the bottom into the rear support. Take care with the location of these screw holes. Glue and screw the rear axle support in place. Note: If you prefer not to have visible screws in the bottom of the wagon just clamp and glue the support to the wagon bottom.

22. Next, fix the axles in place through the axle supports. Apply glue to the centers, insert them through the supports, and center them carefully. If you use metal rod or pipe, an epoxy glue gives the best bond between the wood and metal.

23. All that remains now is to bolt on the handle and the front axle support and attach the wheels. However, it will be easier to paint or finish the wagon before doing this.

First, give all the parts a final finish sanding. Then dust them well. If you want the wagon red, use a good semigloss acrylic enamel. If you have used an attractive wood and prefer a natural finish, a clear satin polyurethane varnish or lacquer looks attractive. Give all parts at least 2 coats of finish.

24. When the last coat of finish is quite dry (a total of 24 hours drying time), complete the assembly. Bolt the front axle support to the wagon, using a ¼-inch by 3-inch bolt. Insert the 1½-inch flat washer between the support and the wagon bottom. Add a lock washer, screw on the nut, and tighten the assembly so that there is no wobble. Bolt the handle onto the yoke, using the ⅛-inch bolt. Lightly peen (using a ball-peen hammer) the bolt end so that the nut will not work itself off.

25. Slide the wheels onto the axles. They should turn freely. If they do not, gently enlarge the holes or add petroleum jelly, soap, or beeswax for lubricant. Tap on the axle end caps to hold the wheels in place.

Materials List

Soft pine was selected for this project because it is light and easy to work. However, this wagon looks especially attractive in a nice hardwood such as hard maple, oak, cherry, or alder with a natural finish. A piece of 1 by 8 lumber, approximately 10 feet long, is required. The 1½-inch-thick axle supports can be cut from a piece of 2 by 6 or made by face-gluing the ¾-inch stock. In any case, the lumber should be relatively free of knots or other defects. All the pieces should come from clear sections of the wood. The bottom and yoke pieces are cut from a 1- by 3-feet piece of ½-inch Baltic birch plywood or the equivalent. The dowel pieces should be hardwood. See Wood Materials, page 11.

Lumber

Piece	No. of Pieces	Thickness	Width	Length
Bottom	1	½" plywood	10½"	20"
Yoke	2	½" plywood	5"	5"
Sides	2	½"	3½"	20"
Handle	1	⅝"	¾"	21"
Ends	2	¾"	3½"	11"
Wheels	4	¾"	6½"	6½"
Outer wheel rims	4	¾"	6½"	6½"
Axle supports	2	1½"	3¾"	7"
Handle grip	1	⅜" dowel		

Hardware and Miscellaneous

Item	Quantity	Size	Description
Pipe, rod, or dowels	2	½" × 9½"	½" OD, for axles
Axle end caps	4	½"	Steel
Bolt	1	¼" × 3"	Carriage bolt with nut, for pivot bolt
Bolt	1	³/₁₆" × 2"	Stove bolt with nut, for handle
Washer	1	¼"	Lock
Washer	1	¼" × 1½"	Flat
Wire brads	20	1"	Finishing
Wire brads	20	1¼"	Finishing
Screws	5	1¼" × #8	Flat head, bright
Wood filler	1 tube or small can		Matching wood color
Glue	1 small bottle		Woodworking or epoxy
Sandpaper	2–3 sheets	100–150 grit	Medium and fine
Finish	1 can		Enamel or clear

MECHANICAL AND RIDING TOYS

S lightly more complex than the projects in the previous chapter, these toys will fascinate children with their motions. The two passengers in the back of the Rumble-Seat Car bounce up and down, the paddle wheel on the ferryboat goes round and round, and the little dog wags its tail and bobs its head as it moves along. The airplane's wheels and propeller spin, and the gear machine illustrates the fundamentals of gear motion.

All children love to rock. Both the riding toys in this chapter are universal favorites; the Pony Rocker and the Rocking Dinosaur are two imaginative versions of the timeless rocking horse.

Most of the projects in this chapter are a bit more complicated than those in the previous chapter, although this Paddle-Wheel Ferryboat is fairly easy to build (see page 66).

RUMBLE-SEAT CAR

This delightful toy shows children how cams work. As the car is pushed or pulled, the two people in the rumble seat bump up and down in opposite directions based upon the setting of the cams inside the car. This project is guaranteed to evoke curiosity from kids ages one and up.

For this project you will need a coping or scroll saw or a jigsaw, saber saw, or band saw with a narrow fine-tooth blade to cut the curved pieces. You need a hole saw or circle cutter to make the wheels.

Power sanding tools, such as a belt sander, a vibrating-pad sander, or a flap wheel sander, help make the sanding job easier. A drill with ⅛-inch, ¼-inch, ⁷/₁₆-inch, and 1-inch bits, a wood rasp, four or more C-clamps, and other ordinary hand tools are also needed. See the comments in Tools and Techniques on page 7.

Building Steps

1. The car body is made up of 5 pieces or laminates: two ¼-inch plywood pieces on the outside and three ¾-inch solid wood pieces on the inside. If you have access to a band saw, saw the outside shape of all these pieces at the same time.

To do this, cut out the blanks for the 2 outside body pieces from the ¼-inch plywood and for the 3 interior body pieces from the ¾-inch solid wood. Cut all these pieces to the squared dimensions shown in the materials list. Stack the pieces, keeping the 2 plywood pieces together and on top, and join them temporarily. For information on how to do this, read Duplicate Sawing or Drilling on page 9. If you decide to use nails, position them in the area where the windows will be cut out.

2. Enlarge the entire outline of the outside body piece, and transfer it to the top piece of plywood in your stack. See Transferring Shapes From Illustrations on page 13. Carefully saw out the outside of this shape. Remember, the smoother the cuts, the less follow-up sanding will be needed.

3. While all the pieces are still stacked, sand them. You may want to start with a medium-rough wood rasp or coarse sandpaper and then move to medium-grit sandpaper. Use a power sander if one is available. Remove all saw marks, and smooth and round the surfaces, but be careful not to round any of the edges or corners.

4. Separate the 2 plywood pieces from the stack, keeping them joined. Separate the 3 interior pieces, taking them apart. Select one of these pieces to be the center piece and copy the outline for the cam cavity from the illustrations. Saw this out.

The driver of this Rumble-Seat Car wisely keeps a close watch on the road, but the passengers in the rear bounce up and down as the car rolls along.

Car Pattern on ½" Squares

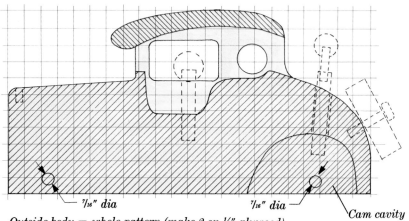

— ⁷⁄₁₆" dia   ⁷⁄₁₆" dia

Cam cavity

Outside body = whole pattern (make 2 on ¼" plywood)

 Interior body (make 3—cut cam cavity from 1)

 Roof

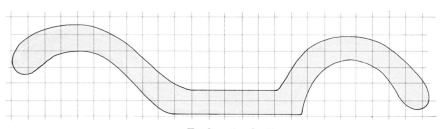

Fenders (make 2)

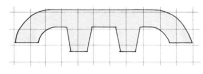

Front bumper

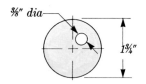

⅜" dia

1¾"

Cam (make 2)

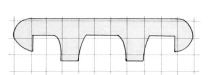

Rear bumper

5. Now reassemble the 3 interior body pieces, placing the one with the cam cavity in the middle. Carefully align all the edges, apply glue, and clamp together. Use small pieces of wood as pads between the clamps and the work to prevent marring. Wipe off any excess glue with a damp rag or sponge.

6. After the glue has dried, remove the clamps. Draw the design of the inner body and roof piece on the wood. Go back to the band saw and first saw off the roof piece in one cut. Do this carefully; you will be using this piece in the assembly. Cut out the dashboard and seat, creating the rest of the interior body shape.

Sand these sawn surfaces smooth. Be careful not to round any of the edges, especially on the roof piece.

7. Next, cut out the window openings in the outside body parts. These 2 pieces of plywood should still be tacked together from the original stack. Draw the window designs, including the location for the 1-inch rear window hole.

Start by boring this 1-inch hole through the 2 pieces of ¼-inch plywood. Use a spur or Forstner bit if you have one. Spade bits tend to tear when used with plywood. Be sure to use a piece of scrap for backup to prevent the bit from tearing the grain when it emerges.

8. Using a ¼-inch drill bit, bore a hole somewhere inside the window cutout for blade access. Using a hand coping saw, a scroll saw, or a saber saw or jigsaw with a narrow fine-cutting blade, saw out this opening. Sand it smooth.

Car Assembly

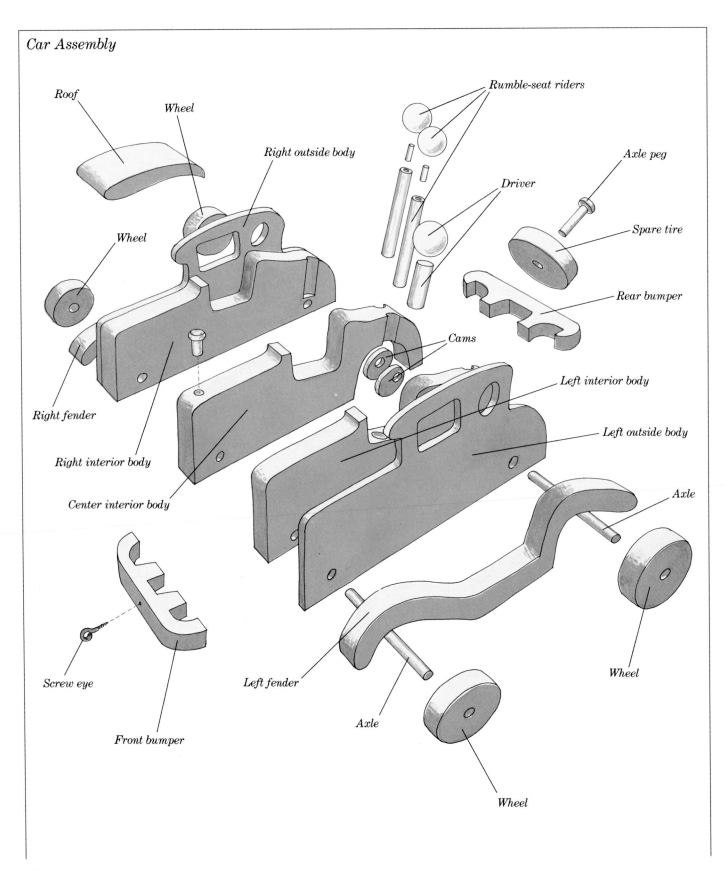

Roof

Wheel

Right outside body

Rumble-seat riders

Axle peg

Driver

Spare tire

Wheel

Rear bumper

Cams

Left interior body

Right fender

Left outside body

Right interior body

Center interior body

Axle

Screw eye

Wheel

Front bumper

Left fender

Axle

Wheel

9. Next, assemble and seat the driver. Start by drilling a ⅜-inch hole at a slight angle, as shown in the illustrations. This is a blind hole about ½ inch deep. Drill another ⅜-inch blind hole into the center of the 1-inch ball (the driver's head).

10. Cut the driver's body from a piece of ⅜-inch dowel. Sand this dowel until it fits snugly but not too tightly into the 2 holes you drilled in the previous step. Whittle a small, flat area ½ inch up both ends of the dowel to allow excess glue to escape as the dowel is tapped into the blind holes. Apply a smear of glue to both ends of the dowel, and tap one end into the wood ball and the other into the hole in the body seat. Wipe off any excess glue.

11. Once the 2 sides and the roof are attached, it may be difficult to paint or finish the driver and the car's interior, especially if you are using a brush. If this is the case, you may want to paint the interior, including the underside of the roof piece, at this time. If you plan to use spray paint, you should be able to paint the insides after final assembly.

12. The complete body can now be assembled. Apply glue, and carefully position the left and right outer body pieces against the sides of the interior body assembly. Clamp, using pads to prevent marring. Tighten the clamps sufficiently to hold the lower part of the assembly in position, apply glue, and slide the roof piece into position between the 2 outer body parts. Use another clamp or two to hold it tightly in position. Tighten all the clamps. Wipe away excess glue.

13. Drill two ⁷⁄₁₆-inch holes at the correct position and angle for the rumble-seat riders. Refer to the illustration for this. These holes go all the way through the body.

The axle holes are also ⁷⁄₁₆ inch and go clear through the body. Drill the axle holes, making sure they are straight and aligned.

Drill a ⁵⁄₁₆-inch hole in the center rear of the body for the spare-tire mount and another ⁵⁄₁₆-inch hole on the front of the hood for the radiator cap. Both these holes are blind, ½ inch deep.

14. Finish shaping and smoothing the car body. Use a rasp or belt sander to finalize the outside shape. If necessary, fill any cracks or voids with wood filler. Let dry, and sand flush. With sandpaper or a flap wheel sander, round all the edges and corners, and smooth the surfaces. Progress from medium- to fine-grit sandpaper.

15. Enlarge the patterns for the 2 fenders and the front and back bumpers, and transfer them to the ¾-inch lumber. See Transferring Shapes From Illustrations on page 13. The grain should run lengthwise. Cut these out. A scroll saw works well for this. Otherwise, use a coping saw or a band saw with a narrow blade. Sand these pieces, rounding all the edges except where they attach to the body.

16. Cut the dowels. Cut the 2 axles from a ⅜-inch dowel. The bodies of the 2 rumble-seat riders are also ⅜-inch dowel stock. Cut the necks of the rumble-seat riders from a piece of ¼-inch dowel. When done, give all these parts a light sanding to remove fuzz and smooth the surfaces.

17. Copy the pattern for the cams onto the ¼-inch plywood, and saw these to shape. Smooth the outside circumference with a rasp or sandpaper or both, slightly rounding the edges. Be careful to remove any nicks or other defects that could cause the rider dowels to catch on the cams.

Drill the off-center ⅜-inch axle hole in each cam. Note that where you drill these holes—and their position on the axle—determines the bounce of the rumble-seat riders.

18. You may prefer to buy pre-turned solid hardwood wheels. If you elect to make your own, use a hole saw or a circle cutter. Use the circle cutter only in a stationary drill press; it is dangerous to use with a hand drill. The wheels in the photograph were made from ¾-inch stock. You may want to use something slightly thinner.

Make 5 wheels. If the hole saw or circle cutter has a ¼-inch center bit, drill these holes out with a ⅜-inch bit. Give each wheel a good sanding, rounding all the edges.

19. To assemble the rumble-seat riders, drill ¼-inch blind holes, ¼ inch deep, into the center of the two ¾-inch wood balls (these are the heads) and into the center of one end of each rider dowel body. Lightly smear glue on each end of the dowel necks, and tap one end into the ball and the other into the dowel. About ¼ inch of neck should still show. Wipe off any excess glue.

20. Predrill through the cams with a ¹⁄₃₂-inch hole to ensure the position of the ⅝-inch brads. For final assembly, slide one end of an axle dowel into the rear axle hole in the body. Slip the 2 cams up into the cam cutout, and slide the axle through the cam holes. Continue to slide the axle through the axle hole until it protrudes evenly on both sides of the body.

Fine-tune the cam positions by sliding them along the axle until each one is directly under a rumble-seat rider's hole. Turn the axle to make sure it still rotates freely. Now put the riders in the rumble seat and experiment with the cam positions until you get the movement you want. Mark the locations on the cam and axle dowel. Temporarily slide the cams out of the way so that you can apply some glue to the axles. Return the cams to their correct position and nail in place using a ⅝-inch brad in each.

21. Attach the fenders to the body with the 1½-inch brads and some glue. It is best to predrill the nail holes through the fenders, using a very small drill bit to reduce the chance of splitting the fender pieces.

Attach the front and back bumpers in the same manner. Use glue and 1¼-inch brads, and predrill the holes.

22. Insert the front axle. Allow some clearance between the wheels and the car sides to prevent binding. Glue the 4 wheels in place.

23. Using the axle peg, attach the spare tire (wheel). Cut the peg to the appropriate length, depending upon the thickness of the tire.

Cut the second axle peg to an appropriate length, apply a small smear of glue, and insert it into the radiator-cap hole.

24. Countersink all the nails, and fill them and any other cracks or mars with wood filler. Sand flush. Sand off any remaining saw or machine marks, round all the corners and edges, and smooth all the surfaces. Dust the toy well when done.

25. If you used an attractive wood, you may want to finish the car with a clear satin finish such as varnish, lacquer, or wax. Otherwise, paint it the color of your choice.

Spray paint goes on easily, dries quickly, and is easy to clean up. With some care and correct positioning of the spray head, you should be able to paint the insides of the car satisfactorily. You may want to practice to determine the correct distance and angle before spraying the real thing. Be sure to read the instructions on the can and use in a well-ventilated location. Give the car 2 or more coats of finish, whatever kind you use.

However you apply the finish, be careful not to overdo the painting around the wheels and rumble-seat riders and their holes. They will stick. Spin the wheels before each coat is dry to keep them free.

26. After the last coat of finish has dried, apply beeswax, candle wax, or soap to the cam edges and the sides of the rumble-seat rider holes.

Materials List

This project is made from a combination of ¼-inch plywood and ¾-inch solid wood. The car in the photo is made with a good-quality hardwood plywood for the outside pieces and soft pine for the rest. You may want to build the Rumble-Seat Car entirely out of hardwood, such as birch, maple, or cherry. For more information on species selection, see Wood Materials, page 11.

You will need a piece of plywood a little larger than 1 foot square. A piece of 1 by 6 (or the hardwood equivalent), dressed to ¾-inch thickness, about 6 feet long, should be sufficient. Cut all the pieces out of clear sections of the lumber. The dowel pieces are hardwood.

Lumber

Piece	*No. of Pieces*	*Thickness*	*Width*	*Length*
Outside body pieces	2	¼″ plywood	5½″	11½″
Cams	2	¼″ plywood	1¾″	1¾″
Interior body pieces	3	¾″	5½″	11½″
Bumpers	2	¾″	1¼″	5½″
Fenders	2	¾″	3″	13″
Wheels	5	¾″	2¼″	2¼″
Riders' necks	2	¼″ dowel	1″	
Driver's body	1	⅜″ dowel	2″	
Axles	2	⅜″ dowel	4¾″	
Riders' bodies	2	⅜″ dowel	2½″	

Hardware and Miscellaneous

Item	*Quantity*	*Size*	*Description*
Wood balls	2	¾″ dia	Riders' heads
Wood ball	1	1″ dia	Driver's head
Axle pegs	2	5/16″ × 1⅞″	Radiator cap and spare tire peg
Wire brads	2	⅝″	Finishing
Wire brads	8	1¼″	Finishing
Wire brads	4	1½″	Finishing
Screw eye	1	3/16″	For pull cord
Plastic cord	1	36″	
Wood filler	1 tube or small can		Matching wood color
Glue	1 small bottle		Woodworking
Sandpaper	2 sheets	100–150 grit	Medium and fine
Finish	1 can		Enamel or clear

MARVELOUS GEAR MACHINE

This project is a conversation piece as well as a toy for children from four to ten years old. It is designed to teach the mechanics of gears and motion. When you turn the handle, all the gears move, the small gears faster than the big ones. The motion is transferred from gear to gear, and at the end the saw moves at the same pace as the first gear.

The task of cutting out the various gears makes this a great project for someone with a scroll saw, but if you enjoy doing slow and intricate work, a hand coping saw can certainly be used. A jigsaw or band saw with a very narrow blade could also do the job.

Use a table saw, if one is available, to cut the dado in the base. Otherwise, you can simply omit the slot and mount the gear housing directly on the base. In the building steps, the first option (using the dado) is referred to as alternative A, and the second is alternative B. Other tools needed include a drill with standard bits under ½ inch and four or more C-clamps. See the comments in Tools and Techniques on page 7.

Two options are given for attaching the gears to the gear housing. The first requires that you slide the gears over fixed axle dowels and hold them in place with screws and washers. In the steps this is referred to as alternative C. The second option is to use turned axle pegs that can be removed. This is alternative D in the building steps.

Building Steps

1. Begin by cutting and assembling the base and gear housing. Using a table saw, if one is available, cut the base from the ¾-inch stock. Next, cut the blanks for the gear housing and gear-housing backup. Note that the backup is cut from ¼-inch plywood. Read step 2 before cutting the final width of these 2 pieces.

2. Alternative A: Mount a dado blade. Cut a ⅜-inch-deep dado groove, 1 inch wide, down the center of the base. This groove will be used to hold the gear-housing assembly. Check the illustrations for details. If you don't have a dado blade (or a table saw), you can make this groove with a router fitted with a straight-shank bit.

Alternative B: You can also omit this groove or slot and simply screw the gear-housing assembly onto the base. Note, however, that if you plan to attach the assembly to the base in this manner, both the gear housing and gear-housing backup should be cut or ripped back to a 9⅜-inch width. Then you can skip step 3.

3. Alternative A: While you are still at the saw, again put on a saw blade and cut the filler block from the same stock from which you sawed the base. Note that this is a ⅜-inch by 1-inch

This gear machine "saws" the little log on the sawhorse when the handle on the first large gear is turned.

piece. This means that 2 rip cuts will have to be made. If you are using a table saw, be sure to use a push stick and hold-downs to protect yourself. Rip the 1-inch width so that the block fits snugly in the dado groove cut in the previous step.

4. The gear-housing assembly consists of a laminate of the ¾-inch gear housing and the ¼-inch gear-housing backup. Get the 2 blanks you sawed in step 1. Glue the pieces together and clamp with C-clamps. Place blocks between the clamps and the piece to spread the pressure and prevent marring. Allow the glue to dry fully before removing the clamps.

5. Transfer the outline of the gear housing from the illustration to this glued piece. See Transferring Shapes From Illustrations on page 13. Cut out the shape of the housing, using a coping or scroll saw. A jigsaw or band saw can also be used if fitted with a narrow blade. Saw the lines carefully to save sanding later on.

6. Very carefully locate the positions of the axle pins on the gear housing. Use an awl to indent the centers of the holes; this will help keep the drill from shifting. Using a brad-pointed drill bit, if available, drill these holes ¼ inch in diameter. Use a backup piece of wood to keep the wood from tearing when the bit emerges.

7. Give the gear housing and the base a good sanding at this time. Before you start, you may want to touch up the shape of the housing with a rasp. Sand out all saw marks, round the edges, and smooth all surfaces. If you used softwood plywood for the backup, there may be some internal voids in the edges. Fill these with wood filler, let them dry, and sand flush.

8. Cut out the 2 sawhorse pieces. Note that these are ⅝ inch square. Saw the ⅝-inch width from the ¾-inch stock, and then rerip to a thickness of ⅝ inch. If you are doing this on a table saw, take care—use a push stick and watch your fingers.

After cutting the sawhorse pieces to length, cut a 30-degree angle on the ends of each piece so they sit flat on the base. Next, use a rasp to shape out one side of each piece at the top, as shown in the drawing. This will give the sawhorse a better hold on the log piece. You may also want to notch each sawhorse piece so that they fit together better. Use a fine-tooth handsaw and/or chisel and cut a notch ⅝-inch wide by ⁵⁄₁₆-inch deep.

9. Cut the saw out at this time. Note that the saw blank is only ⅛ inch thick but 1 inch wide. Again, 2 rip cuts will be required. First saw a 1-inch-wide piece from your ¾-inch stock, and then rip a ⅛-inch strip off the side. Be sure to watch your fingers and use a push stick.

Review the illustration of the saw piece, and then do the final shaping with a rasp, plane, or belt sander. You can draw serrations on the bottom edge of the saw with black felt pen after finishing the toy, or you can cut serrations on the bottom edge now. These will cause it to bounce a little as it passes back and forth through the log. Sand the saw piece smooth when done.

10. Cut all the dowel pieces to length. This includes the gear handle and saw spacer block. Sand one end of the handle round.

For alternative C, saw the gear axle pins to length. Alternative D uses ¼-inch preturned wheel axle pegs instead. (See Sources on page 13.) These can be inserted through the gears and fit into the gear housing. Alternative D allows the gears to be removed, presenting a challenge to the child to get all the gears back in their correct location. With alternative C, the gears are fixed in place.

Finally, cut the log piece. This can be a piece of 1-inch dowel or a short piece of a tree branch or limb, about 1 inch in diameter, with the bark still on it. Cut to final length. Using a handsaw, cut a kerf slot in the log to hold the saw. See the illustrations for the correct location. Enlarge the slot, if necessary, so that the saw moves easily in it.

11. Alternative C: If you are using dowels for the gear axle pins, this is a good time to glue them to the gear housing. Apply glue, and tap them in from the solid wood side until the dowel is just flush with the plywood backup piece. Wipe off any excess glue with a damp rag. If you are using the removable axle pegs (alternative D), omit this step.

12. Glue the sawhorse pieces together, and then glue them to the gear housing. Glue the log in place. Wipe off any excess glue.

13. Alternative A: To attach the gear-housing assembly to the base, drill three ³⁄₁₆-inch pilot holes down through the center of the dado groove and through the base. Follow the illustrations. Countersink the holes on the bottom. Position the assembly in the dado groove, and finish the pilot holes by drilling ⅛-inch holes up into the assembly. Glue the assembly in place, pulling it tight with the 1-inch #8 flat-head screws.

Alternative B: If you elected not to cut the dado, simply screw the assembly onto the base. Use three 1½-inch #8 flat-head screws. Drill countersunk screw pilot holes as described in the previous paragraph. Apply glue, and screw the assembly in place.

14. Alternative A: If you used the dado-groove assembly technique, the empty dado grooves need to be filled with the filler block you cut in step 3. Cut the block to the proper length, apply glue, and insert it in the empty groove. Wipe off any excess glue with a damp rag.

15. You are now ready to start on the gears, the heart of this project. Begin by cutting out all the gear blanks from the ½-inch stock to the dimensions shown in the materials list. Make sure they are square.

Gear Machine Pattern

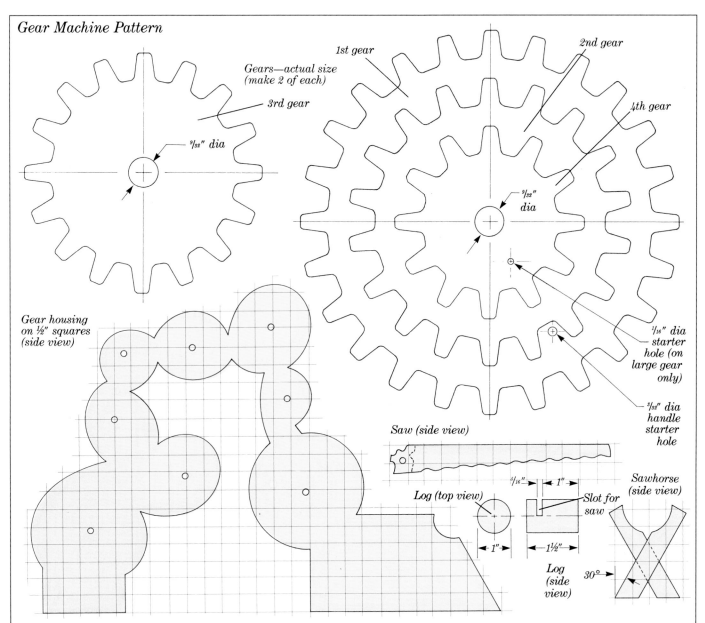

Gears—actual size (make 2 of each)

1st gear
2nd gear
3rd gear
4th gear

⁹/₃₂" dia

⁹/₃₂" dia

¹/₁₆" dia starter hole (on large gear only)

⁵/₃₂" dia handle starter hole

Gear housing on ½" squares (side view)

Saw (side view)

Log (top view)

Sawhorse (side view)

Slot for saw

⁴/₁₆"   1"

1"   1½"

Log (side view)   30°

Temporarily join the gear pairs, using one of the techniques recommended in Duplicate Sawing or Drilling on page 9. This permits you to saw and shape 2 gears at once. Do not use double-stick tape in this particular application.

16. Draw diagonal lines from the corners to locate the centers, and mark these well. Carefully trace the gear designs from the illustrations, indicating the centers, and transfer the pattern to the gear blanks. Use a pin to match the center of the pattern to the exact center of the piece.

17. Using a coping or scroll saw, slowly and carefully cut out the teeth. As mentioned, you can use a band saw with a ⅛-inch fine-tooth blade.

18. After you have sawn the teeth as finely as you can, refine their shapes with a file or fine rasp. Do this in a vise, protecting the gear pieces from damage by the jaws if you are using a metal vise. Finish the shaping and smooth the teeth with sandpaper.

19. After the gear pairs are shaped to your satisfaction, drill the gear axle holes. First, drill a test hole in some scrap using a ⁹/₃₂-inch bit, brad pointed if possible. See how the ¼-inch axle dowels or pegs fit in this hole. You want the fit to be loose enough for the gear to turn freely but snug enough to prevent wobble. You may have to move down to a ¼-inch or up to a ⁵/₁₆-inch hole. Drill the holes through the center points in the paired gears.

Gear Machine Assembly

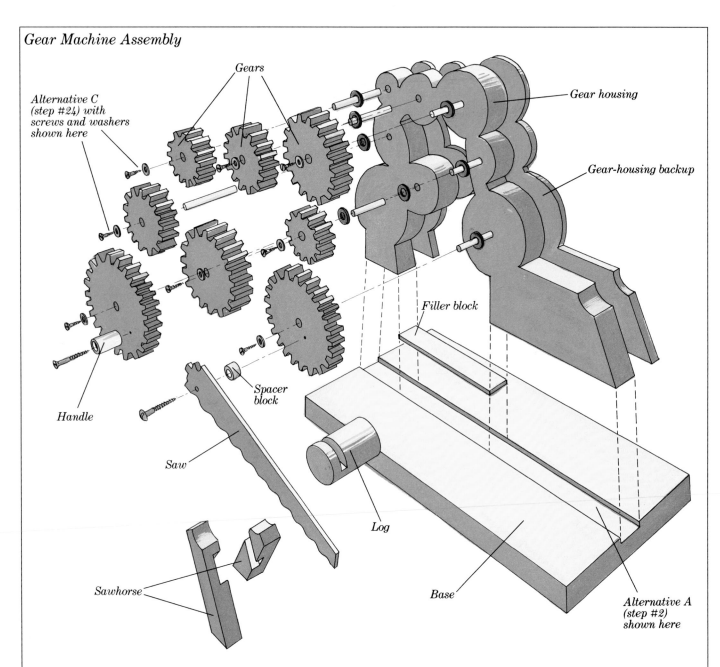

Gears

Alternative C
(step #24) with
screws and washers
shown here

Gear housing

Gear-housing backup

Filler block

Handle

Spacer block

Saw

Log

Sawhorse

Base

Alternative A
(step #2)
shown here

20. Separate the gear pairs. Give the individual gears a final sanding. Drill starter holes in the 2 big gears for the #8 handle screw and the #4 saw screw. Use a very small ¹/₁₆-inch bit for the saw screw and a slightly larger ³/₃₂-inch bit for the handle screw, taking care with each not to drill all the way through the ½-inch-thick gear. Locate these holes from the illustrations.

21. Alternative C: If you are using fixed axle pins, drill starter holes in the ends of the dowel pins for the #3 screws that hold the gears in place. Use a small ¹/₁₆-inch bit. Locate the centers of the dowels with a pencil, then indent them with an awl before drilling.

22. Drill a ¼-inch hole in the end of the ½-inch dowel handle to a depth of ¼ inch. This is to recess the head of the handle screw. Mark and

indent the location before drilling. Drill another ⁷/₃₂-inch hole clear through the center of the handle dowel. Attach the handle to the gear, using the 1¼-inch #8 brass round-head handle screw. Loosen the screw just enough so that the handle turns freely. Check the back side of the gear. If the screw point has come through, file it flush.

23. Drill a ⅛-inch hole through the center of the spacer dowel. Check to make sure the #4 saw screw moves freely through it. Enlarge the hole if necessary with a larger bit. Drill a hole of the same diameter in the correct position through the handle end of the saw. Attach the saw and spacer to the large gear with the ¾-inch #4 brass round-head saw screw. Loosen the screw just enough so that the saw moves freely.

24. Assemble the gears on the base-housing assembly. Consult the illustrations for details. Alternative C: If you are using fixed axle pins, a ¼-inch brass washer goes on first, then the gear, then a small brass washer, and finally the ¼-inch #3 brass retainer screw.

Alternative D: If you are using axle pegs, insert the pegs through the gears, add ¼-inch washers, and then push the pegs into the holes in the gear housing. You may need to sand the ends of the pegs lightly if the fit is too tight.

25. You will probably need to make some adjustments with a fine file, sandpaper, and a screwdriver. When everything turns and moves to your satisfaction, remove all the detachable parts. Sand everything once more with the finest-grit sandpaper you have, and dust well.

26. Your original selection of woods will probably determine whether you paint this project or give it a natural finish. You may want to combine different colors for the gears or use a combination of clear finish and paint. In any case, all the parts should have at least 2 coats. Spray paint is the easiest to use. Be sure to cover the gear axles and the dowel ends of the axle pegs with masking tape to prevent paint buildup, which could inhibit the free movement of the gears.

27. After the finish is completely dry, reassemble the gears and give the toy a whirl.

Materials List

Baltic birch plywood, tempered hardboard, or solid hardwood, ¼-inch thick, can be used. The project photographed is built of solid oak. One square foot should do the job with some to spare. The other pieces are cut from pieces of ¾-inch lumber. You can glue-up the wide piece required for the gear housing, if necessary. Hardwood is recommended, but pine or other even-textured softwoods can be used. See Wood Materials, page 11.

A piece of ¼-inch plywood, 10 by 15 inches, is needed to back up and strengthen the gear housing. Use Baltic birch or another hardwood plywood, if you have a piece handy. The log can be made from either a piece of 1-inch dowel or a section of a branch with bark. All the dowel pieces should be hardwood.

The longer mounting screws are needed if you do not cut the dado in the base. The axle pegs permit removal of the gears. If you use these, the eight #3 retainer screws and small brass washers are not needed.

Lumber

Piece	No. of Pieces	Thickness	Width	Length
Saw	1	⅛"	1"	6¾"
Gear-housing backup	1	¼" plywood	10"	15"
Filler block (alternative A)	1	⅜"	1"	5¾"
Gears, fourth	2	½"	2¼"	2¼"
Gears, third	2	½"	2¾"	2¾"
Gears, second	2	½"	3¼"	3¼"
Gears, first	2	½"	4¼"	4¼"
Gear housing	1	¾"	10"	15"
Base	1	¾"	6⅞"	14⅛"
Sawhorse	2	⅝"	⅝"	3"
Log	1	1" dowel or branch	1½"	
Gear axle pins (alternative C)	8	¼" dowel	1¼"	
Gear handle	1	½" dowel	1"	
Saw spacer block	1	½" dowel	⅜"	

Hardware and Miscellaneous

Item	Quantity	Size	Description
Axle pegs	8	¼" × 1½"	For alternative D
Screws, retainer	8	¼" × #3	Brass, round head, for alternative C
Screw, saw	1	¾" × #4	Brass, round head
Screws, mounting	3	1" × #8	Brass, flat head, for alternative A
Screw, handle	1	1¼" × #8	Brass, round head
Screws, mounting	3	1½" × #8	Brass, flat head, for alternative B
Washers	8	For #3 screws	Brass, for alternative C
Washers	8	¼"	Brass
Glue	1 bottle		Woodworking
Wood filler	1 tube or small can		Matching wood color
Sandpaper	2 sheets	100–150 grit	Medium and fine
Finish	1 can		Enamel or clear

PADDLE-WHEEL FERRYBOAT

*T*his little ferryboat is a delightful pull toy for one- to three-year-olds. It rolls on wheels and is meant to be towed on dry land by young ferryboat captains.

You can make this project with common hand tools, including a coping saw, jigsaw, or saber saw, and a drill with ⅛-inch, ¼-inch, ¹⁷⁄₆₄-inch or ⁵⁄₁₆-inch, and 1-inch bits. A wood rasp, a flat file, a drawing compass, and several medium-sized C-clamps are also needed.

If available, stationary power tools, including a drill press and a table saw, a scroll saw, or a band saw with a narrow blade, would facilitate the construction. See the comments in Tools and Techniques on page 7.

Building Steps

1. Start by sawing all the wood parts to square dimensions. Use a table or radial arm saw if one is available. Cut the top deck and the paddles from the ¼-inch plywood. Cut the hull, the wheelhouse, the axle blocks, and the 2 cabin parts from ¾-inch stock. Note that you need to cut 2 pieces for the cabin to make the 1½-inch thickness. Make these 2 pieces slightly oversized and then cut them to final size after gluing them together.

The paddle wheel on this simple ferryboat revolves as the toy is pulled forward on its four wheels.

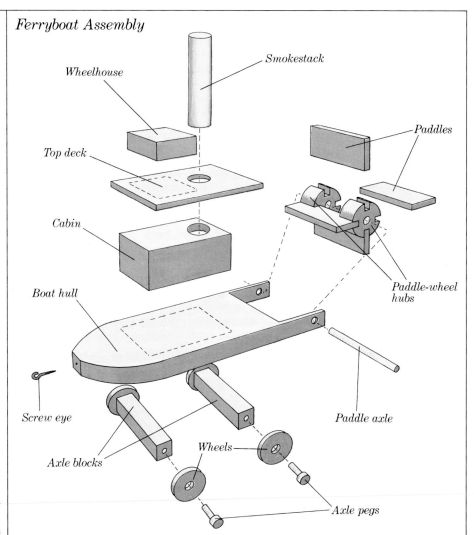

Ferryboat Assembly

Wheelhouse

Smokestack

Top deck

Paddles

Cabin

Paddle-wheel hubs

Boat hull

Paddle axle

Screw eye

Wheels

Axle blocks

Axle pegs

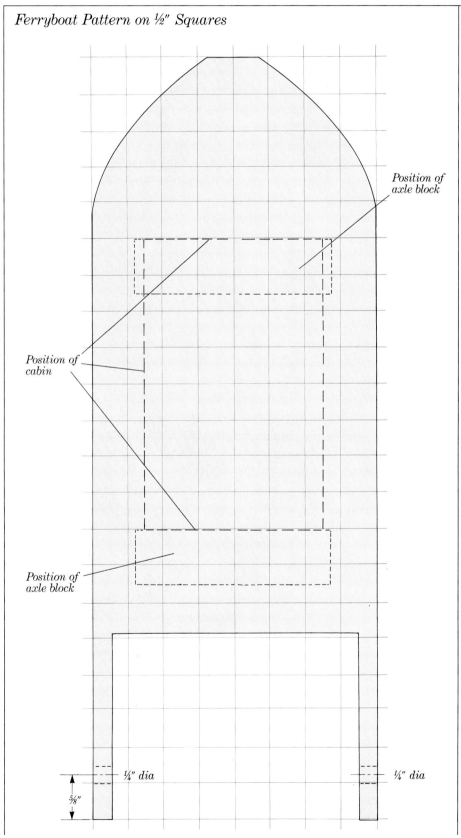

Ferryboat Pattern on ½″ Squares

Position of axle block

Position of cabin

Position of axle block

¼″ dia

¼″ dia

⅝″

2. Face-glue the 2 cabin pieces and clamp together. Use pads under the clamps to spread the pressure and prevent marring. After the glue has set, cut the cabin to final size.

3. Shape the hull as shown in the illustrations. Rough-cut the pointed bow and the paddle-wheel cutout, using a coping or band saw. Finish and smooth the cuts with a rasp or sandpaper or both.

4. Sand all the flat surfaces of these cut pieces at this time. Be careful, however, not to round any edges.

5. Cut out the 2 blanks for the paddle-wheel hubs. To locate the centers, quarter the pieces by drawing diagonal lines from the corners. Using a drawing compass, set the radius for $^{13}/_{16}$ inch, and draw a $1^{5}/_{8}$-inch-diameter circle on each. Saw out these circles with a coping or band saw, and then sand them smooth and round. If you have a $1^{5}/_{8}$-inch hole saw or circle cutter, you can use it instead. Use the circle cutter only in a drill press.

6. Drill a $^{17}/_{64}$-inch hole in the center of each of the hubs. A $^{5}/_{16}$-inch hole will also work. If the hole saw or circle cutter already drilled a ¼-inch hole, simply enlarge it. Next, using the diagonal lines as centerlines, cut 4 notches, slightly less than ¼ inch wide and ⅜ inch deep. With the sanded ¼-inch plywood paddle blades in hand, file out the width of the notches until the blades fit snugly. Use a flat, mill-bastard file for this.

7. Cut the dowels to length for the ¼-inch-diameter paddle-wheel axle and the 1-inch-diameter smokestack. Sand them lightly.

8. Drill a ¼-inch hole through the sides of the tabs on the rear of the hull for the paddle-wheel axle. Consult the illustrations for the correct location. Use a drill press if one is available. With luck, the drill bit will be long enough to pass through both tabs. If it is not, drill from both sides. Be careful to keep the holes aligned and straight.

Drill ¼-inch holes through the axle blocks. Again, try to keep them straight and square. The last hole, for the smokestack, will be made later.

9. Begin the assembly, starting with the paddle wheel. Slip the 2 hubs on the ¼-inch axle dowel to help keep everything aligned. Glue the 4 paddle blades in the slots of the hubs. You can use several rubber bands as clamps while the glue is drying. Wipe off any excess glue with a damp rag.

10. Position, glue, and clamp the 2 axle blocks in place on the bottom of the hull.

11. Apply some glue to the bottom of the cabin, and nail it in position on the hull. Use the 1½-inch finishing nails, driving them through the bottom of the hull into the cabin. Clamp if necessary.

12. Apply some glue to the top deck, and nail it in position on top of the cabin. Use 1-inch finishing nails. Be careful not to place a nail where the smokestack hole will be. Apply some glue to the wheelhouse, and nail it in position on the top deck.

13. Drill a 1-inch blind hole, ¾ inch deep, down through the top deck and into the cabin. This is for the smokestack. Use a spur or Forstner-type bit to get a clean hole. If all you have is a spade bit, drill carefully. It tends to tear plywood. You might want to drill this hole at a slight backward angle to give the smokestack some rake. Smear some glue on the smokestack, and insert it in the hole.

14. At this time, give all the parts, including the paddle-wheel assembly, a good sanding. Remove all saw marks, round the sharp edges and corners, and smooth the surfaces.

15. Rotate the paddle wheel on its axle. If it is stiff, slightly sand the ¼-inch dowel until the paddle wheel turns freely. Insert the dowel through one of the hull tabs, through the paddle wheel, and into the other hull tab. Glue the axle to the tabs.

16. Insert an axle peg through each wheel, put some glue on the ends, and then tap them into the holes in the axle blocks.

17. Give the assembly one last sanding and apply a finish. Give the boat at least 2 coats of a natural finish, or paint it the color of your choice. Spray paint goes on easily and involves almost no cleanup. However, be sure to use the spray can in a well-ventilated location. You may want to paint your child's name on the sides or bow of the boat after the finish has dried.

18. After all paint or finish is dried, screw the eye into the prow of the hull. Tie the plastic pull cord to this.

Materials List

This paddle-wheel boat project is made from a short piece of ¾-inch-thick wood such as a 1 by 6. Soft pine will work well, as would an attractive hardwood. Cut all pieces out of clear sections of the lumber. A piece of 1 by 6, 3 to 4 feet long, should do the job. Note that 1 piece is 1½ inches thick. You can make it by gluing 2 pieces of ¾-inch stock together.

This project also calls for some small pieces of ¼-inch plywood. Baltic birch plywood would be best, if you have a piece around, but AC-grade softwood plywood will certainly work. About ½ square foot is required. The short dowel pieces are hardwood. See Wood Materials, page 11.

Lumber

Piece	No. of Pieces	Thickness	Width	Length
Top deck	1	¼″ plywood	4″	4¾″
Paddles	4	¼″ plywood	1⅜″	2½″
Hull	1	¾″	4″	10½″
Wheelhouse	1	¾″	1¾″	2½″
Axle blocks	2	¾″	⅞″	3¼″
Paddle-wheel hubs	2	¾″	2″	2″
Cabin	1	1½″	2½″	4″
Paddle-wheel axle	1	¼″ dowel	4″	
Smokestack	1	1″ dowel	3¾″	

Hardware and Miscellaneous

Item	Quantity	Size	Description
Wood wheels	4	3/16″ × 1¼″	With ¼″ axle holes
Axle pegs	4	¼″ × 1⅜″	
Nails	4	1″	Bright, finishing
Nails	12	1½″	Bright, finishing
Screw eye	1	Small	
Plastic cord	1	36″	
Glue	1 small bottle		Woodworking
Sandpaper	2 sheets	100–150 grit	Medium and fine
Finish	1 can		Enamel or clear

MECHANICAL AIRPLANE

*T*his mechanical toy is fun to make, and it is an easy lesson for your four- to seven-year-old in the application of a drive shaft, belt, and pulley combination. As the wheels turn, a rubber band on the axle makes the propeller move. This toy could easily be adapted as a wind toy or whirligig for your backyard.

You will need a good curve-cutting saw, preferably a band saw. A coping saw, jigsaw, or scroll saw will also do the job. A drill press will be useful for boring the many holes. A number of the pieces are ⅝ inch thick or less. If you plan to machine this thickness yourself, you need, at the minimum, a table saw.

Other tool requirements include ⅛-inch, ¼-inch, 5/16-inch, ⅜-inch, 7/16-inch, ½-inch, and ¾-inch drill bits, a chisel, a wood rasp, some C-clamps, a hot-melt glue gun, and ordinary hand tools. See the comments in Tools and Techniques on page 7.

Building Steps

1. Almost all the parts for this mechanical airplane toy are either ½ inch or ⅝ inch thick. If you are working from standard 1-by or 4/4 stock, which is ¾ inch thick, the first step is to machine the lumber down to the required thicknesses. In this case, planing the ¾-inch lumber is by far the best way to do this. If you don't have access to a planer, have the work done at a local cabinet shop. You can also resaw to the needed thicknesses with a table or band saw. Read Cutting Thin Stock on page 8 for other alternatives.

2. Building the airplane fuselage is probably the trickiest part of this toy project, so start with it. Saw out the 3 fuselage blanks, the center and the 2 side pieces, from ⅝-inch-thick material. Use a band saw if at all possible; otherwise, you can use the following technique with other tools that saw curves.

3. Using several very small drops of hot-melt adhesive, carefully align the edges of the blanks and temporarily tack the 3 pieces together into a single block. Trace the fuselage shapes onto the stack. See Transferring Shapes From Illustrations on page 13. You can either draw the shapes directly on the stacked blanks or enlarge them on a piece of thin cardboard or poster board and then cut them out and use them as patterns. Draw the top pattern on the edges of the stack, spanning the 3 pieces, and draw the side pattern on the side of one of the pieces.

4. Using the pattern drawn on the top of the stack, make the 2 side cuts, tapering to the tail. Try to make these cuts as clean and smooth as possible, so that 2 intact pieces of scrap remain. When you are done, tack these 2 pieces back on, using a small drop or two of hot-melt adhesive, so that the stacked block is square again.

With the reconstituted block on its side, saw out the top and bottom shapes. Remove the side scraps, scraping away any residual glue.

5. While the fuselage is still together, sand all the sawn surfaces smooth. Start with medium-grit sandpaper and finish with fine-grit sandpaper. Pry the 3 pieces apart, and clean off any remaining adhesive.

6. Make the required cutout in the center fuselage piece, as shown in the illustration.

7. Checking the illustration for details, carefully drill a 7/16-inch propeller-shaft hole into the front of the

As the wheels turn, the propeller on this airplane spins, readying it for a transatlantic flight to exotic lands.

center fuselage piece. This hole needs to be 4½ inches deep or deeper. Note that this propeller shaft hole passes through and into the back of the cutout.

8. Cut the propeller shaft from a ⅜-inch dowel. Lightly sand the shaft, rounding the back end with sandpaper. Insert this in the shaft hole in the center fuselage piece, and check to see that it rotates freely.

9. Drill a ⅛-inch hole through the side of the center fuselage, carefully positioning it so that it grazes and cuts a groove near the end of the dowel. As you can see from the illustration, this is to permit the insertion of a ⅛-inch dowel pin to lock the propeller shaft in; the dowel pin prevents it from pulling or falling out, yet still allows it to rotate.

If at all possible, use a drill press for this step. Insert the rounded end of the propeller shaft dowel into the hole in the fuselage center piece. After carefully locating the pin hole, clamp the piece to the drill press table. Drill through just far enough to cut into the side of the dowel, then continue another ⅛ inch. Lock the drill press quill in position but leave the drill running. Slowly rotate the propeller-shaft dowel so that the side of the drill cuts a groove completely around the shaft. Release the quill and withdraw the drill. Unclamp the piece from the table and remove the propeller shaft.

10. Using sandpaper or a very small rat-tail file, smooth and slightly enlarge the groove in the shaft.

11. Cut a short piece of ⅛-inch dowel, about 1½ inches long, for the propeller-shaft pin. Sand it until it fits snugly but slides easily in and out of the hole drilled into the side of the center fuselage piece. Insert the propeller shaft, then insert the shaft pin. Test to see if the shaft rotates easily but is held in place by the pin. If need be, remove the pin and shaft and sand a little more on the groove until it rotates freely.

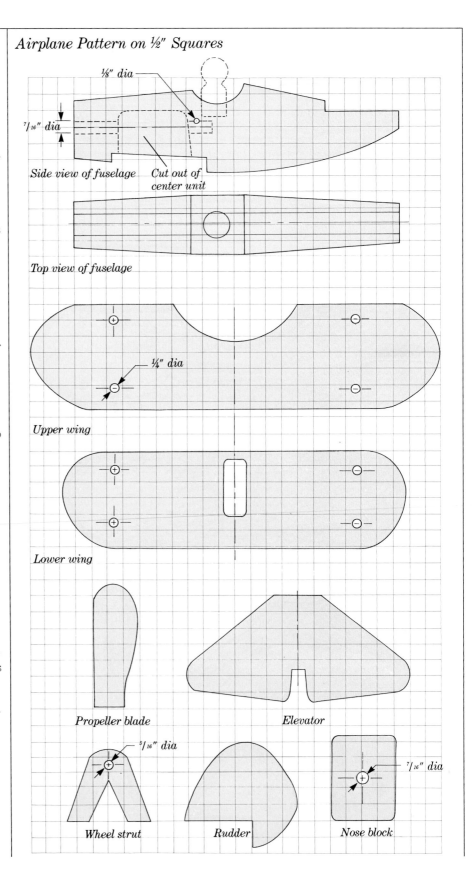

Airplane Pattern on ½" Squares

⅛" dia

⁷/₁₆" dia

Side view of fuselage *Cut out of center unit*

Top view of fuselage

¼" dia

Upper wing

Lower wing

Propeller blade *Elevator*

⁵/₁₆" dia

Wheel strut *Rudder* ⁷/₁₆" dia *Nose block*

12. Coat the propeller shaft and the shaft hole with beeswax or candle wax for lubricant. Reinsert the shaft and lock it in place by tapping in the locking pin. Clip off the excess pin with a pair of wire snippers, and sand it flush. It is not necessary to glue the pin in place. The 2 fuselage side pieces will hold it in position.

13. Cut a strip of medium-grit or fine-grit sandpaper to 1¼ inches by 2 inches. Glue it around the propeller shaft, inside the cutout. Use pins to hold it in place while the glue dries, and then trim it smooth with a razor blade.

14. Now attach the side fuselage pieces to the center piece. Glue, carefully position, and clamp this assembly. Use woodworking glue. Be sure to place pads under the clamps to avoid marring the sides of the fuselage. Clean off any excess glue with a damp rag or sponge.

15. Widen the recess in the center piece to facilitate threading the rubber band drive. Use a chisel for this. Carefully cut the sides of the recess about ¼-inch deep into both of the outside fuselage pieces, widening the hole to 1¼-inch overall. If you have spur bits, drill two ⅜-inch holes into each side piece to the depth of the recess. Clean out with the chisel.

16. Drill a blind ¾-inch hole in the cockpit cutout for the pilot-body dowel. It should be approximately 1 inch deep. Drill a blind ¼-inch hole on the fuselage bottom near the tail for the tail-drag dowel. Angle the hole as shown in the illustrations; it should be about ½ inch deep.

17. Finish the fuselage by sanding all the surfaces flush and smooth. You may need to start with a rasp or belt sander. Round all the corners and edges, except around the cutouts for the wings and elevator.

18. Now get the ½-inch stock you prepared at the start of the project. Lay out the 2 wings, the 2 wheel struts, the elevator, and the rudder, and cut these out. Note that there will be some cross grain in the struts. This will probably not present any major weaknesses, but if you desire, you can cut the wheel struts from small pieces of ½-inch plywood for greater strength.

19. Cut the nose block and a blank for the propeller spinner from the ⅝-inch stock.

20. Cut blanks for the 2 propeller blades. These are ⅛ inch thick and 1⅝ inches wide, so you will have to rip some ¾-inch stock to a width of 1⅝ inches and then rerip to a ⅛-inch thickness. Be very careful here. If you use a table saw, use a push stick and watch your fingers. As an alternative, you can usually find ⅛-inch-thick material at a hobby shop.

21. Cut all the dowel pieces to length. The 4 wing struts, the tail drag, the axle, and the pilot's neck are all cut from ¼-inch dowel stock. The pilot body and the axle pulley are ¾-inch dowels.

22. Position and center the lower wing on top of the upper wing. Securely clamp these 2 pieces together. Locate the wing-strut holes from the illustrations. Drill the four ¼-inch holes down through the lower wing and partially into the upper wing. Do this on a drill press if possible, setting the stop so that the blind holes in the upper wing are ¼ inch deep.

23. Separate the wings and drill two ¾-inch holes in the correct position in the center of the lower wing. Use a piece of scrap wood underneath to keep the drill from splitting the wood when it emerges. Enlarge this hole with a coping saw or jigsaw to the shape shown in the illustration. Sand the edges of the hole smooth.

24. Drill the axle holes in the correct position on the wheel struts. These are ⁵⁄₁₆-inch-diameter holes.

Drill a ⁷⁄₁₆-inch hole through the center of the nose block. Drill a ⅜-inch hole through the center of the spinner blank.

Drill a ¼-inch hole through the center of the axle-pulley dowel, taking care to center it and drill straight.

Drill a blind ¼-inch hole into the center of the wood ball for the pilot's head, and another one down into one end of the pilot's body dowel. Both of these holes are ½ inch deep.

25. Sand all the different pieces, with the exception of the spinner. Remove all saw marks, round the edges, and smooth the surfaces.

26. Now you can begin assembling the airplane. Start by attaching the rudder to the elevator. Use glue and the ⅝-inch brads. Clean off any excess glue with a damp rag.

Slip the nose block onto the propeller shaft and attach it to the front of the fuselage, using glue and brads. Use glue sparingly so that none gets on the propeller shaft. Make sure the shaft still turns freely.

27. Position the 2 wheel struts correctly on the bottom of the wing, and glue and nail them in place. It might be a good idea to insert the axle through the struts during this assembly to ensure that it turns freely.

28. Find the axle-pulley dowel. Wrap a piece of 1⅝-inch by 3-inch sandpaper around it and glue the paper in place, as you did with the propeller shaft. Trim the sandpaper when the glue is dry.

Apply some glue inside the hole in the axle pulley. Slip the wheel axle through one of the struts, through the axle pulley, and then through the other strut, centering the assembly. Wipe off any excess glue, and make sure the axle assembly turns easily.

29. Now finish the wing assembly. Glue and tap the ¼-inch dowel struts into the holes in the lower wing until they are flush with the bottom surface. Align the struts with the blind holes in the upper wing, and tap them home. Be careful to use only a thin smear of glue on the ends of each of the dowels.

Airplane Assembly

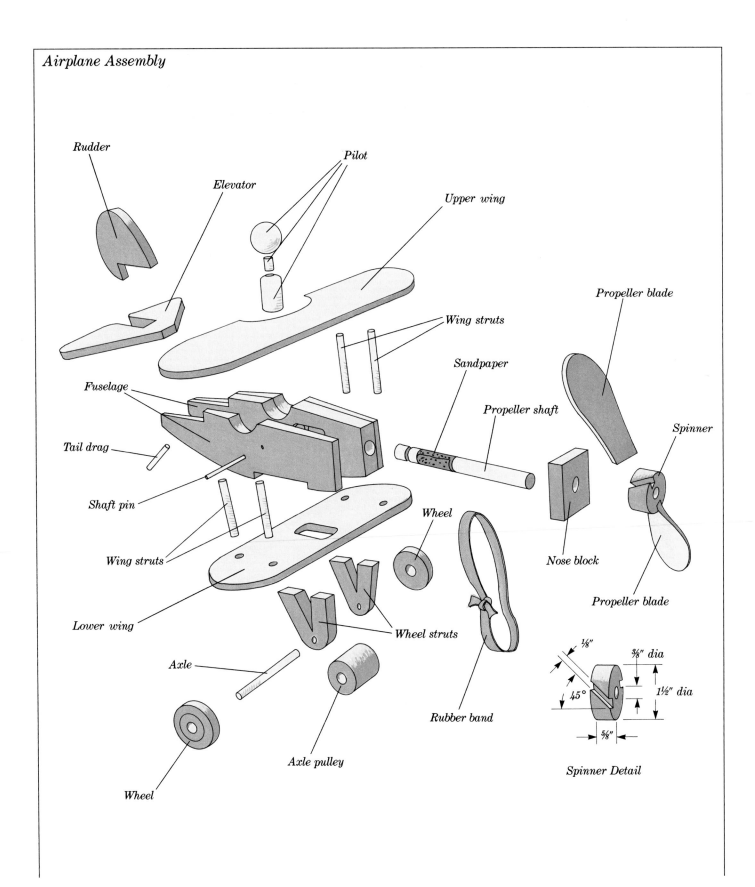

Rudder

Elevator

Pilot

Upper wing

Wing struts

Sandpaper

Propeller blade

Fuselage

Propeller shaft

Spinner

Tail drag

Shaft pin

Wheel

Wing struts

Nose block

Lower wing

Propeller blade

Wheel struts

Axle

Rubber band

Axle pulley

Wheel

⅛"

⅜" dia

45°

1½" dia

⅝"

Spinner Detail

30. While the wing assembly is drying, assemble the pilot. If you have not already done so, round the bored end of the pilot's body dowel with sandpaper. Apply a smear of glue to the pilot's neck dowel, and tap it into the body hole. Apply a smear of glue to the other end of the neck, and tap it into the wood head ball.

After the assembled pilot has dried, see how it fits in the cockpit hole. It should slide in and out easily. You may have to do some additional sanding to the body to get the fit just right.

31. Apply a smear of glue to the end of the tail-drag dowel, and tap it into the hole in the rear of the fuselage. After the glue has set, sand or rasp the end of the dowel to the correct slope.

32. Finally, position both the wing and the rudder-elevator assemblies on the fuselage. Glue and nail in place. Clean off any excess glue.

33. After everything has dried, go over the entire assembly and gently countersink all the visible brads. Fill these with wood filler. When the filler has dried, sand flush. Give the entire airplane assembly a final sanding.

34. The propeller assembly is the last step. First, shape the propeller blades from the ⅛-inch blanks cut in step 19. A sharp knife works well here. Sand the blades smooth.

With the spinner blank in hand, cut two ⅛-inch slots opposite each other, slanted at a 45-degree angle, ½ inch deep, to accept the ends of the propellers. See the illustrations. Either make these cuts by hand or carefully saw them on the band saw.

Shape and sand the spinner round. Glue the propeller blades in place.

35. Glue the propeller assembly onto the end of the propeller shaft. Allow some clearance with the nose block. Check to be sure that everything turns freely.

36. Glue the 2 wheels onto the ends of the wheel axle. Again, check to make sure everything turns freely.

37. To make the rubber-band drive, cut a fairly wide rubber band, loop it around the axle pulley and the propeller shaft, and tie the ends together. The tension is critical; it must not be too tight or too loose. You will have to experiment with this. The plane in the photograph has a ¼-inch-wide rubber band with a small knot tied in it to give the desired tension. The wider the rubber band

the better. A strip of rubber from a discarded bicycle inner tube would also work well for this.

The propeller should spin easily as the airplane rolls along the floor.

38. Dust off the entire airplane. You can paint the plane or use a clear finish if your wood grain is attractive. Hand-painting with a small brush works fine, or simply use spray paint. Give the entire airplane several coats.

Be careful not to get too much paint around the moving parts. If you do, the propeller shaft and the wheel axles will stick tight. Give these parts a spin before the paint has dried. Use masking tape if necessary. Paint lightly around the pilot. It should be easy to remove.

Materials List

You can build this toy in an even-textured softwood or an attractive hardwood. See Wood Materials, page 11. You will need approximately 6 to 8 feet of 1 by 6 (or the hardwood equivalent). This assumes that you reduce the ¾-inch stock to the required ⅛-inch, ½-inch, and ⅝-inch thicknesses. All the pieces should be reasonably free of knots. The dowels and wheels should be hardwood.

Lumber

Piece	No. of Pieces	Thickness	Width	Length
Propeller blades	2	⅛″	1⅝″	4″
Upper wing	1	½″	3¼″	13″
Lower wing	1	½″	3″	11″
Wheel struts	2	½″	2¼″	2⅝″
Elevator	1	½″	3½″	7¼″
Rudder	1	½″	3½″	3¾″
Fuselage	3	⅝″	3″	10¼″
Nose block	1	⅝″	2″	2½″
Spinner	1	⅝″	1½″	1½″
Propeller-shaft pin	1	⅛″ dowel	1½″	
Wing struts	4	¼″ dowel	4¼″	
Axle	1	¼″ dowel	4¼″	
Tail drag	1	¼″ dowel	2″	
Pilot's neck	1	¼″ dowel	1¼″	
Propeller shaft	1	⅜″ dowel	6″	
Axle pulley	1	¾″ dowel	1¾″	
Pilot's body	1	¾″ dowel	1½″	

Hardware and Miscellaneous

Item	Quantity	Size	Description
Wood wheels	2	⁷⁄₁₆″ × 2″	With ¼″ axle holes
Wood ball	1	1″ dia	For pilot's head
Rubber band	1	3″ × 1″	For the belt drive
Wire brads	10	⅝″	Finishing
Wood filler	1 tube or small can		Matching wood color
Glue	1 small bottle		Woodworking
Adhesive	1 stick		Hot melt
Sandpaper	2–3 sheets	100–150 grit	Medium and fine
Finish	1 can		Enamel or clear

PONY ROCKER

All little children, from ages one to four, love rocking horses. This is a heritage design. It is a project that will be passed down from generation to generation.

Almost all the pieces in this traditional design are curved shapes, calling for the use of a band saw. However, a jigsaw or saber saw could be used if a band saw is not available. A drill equipped with ½-inch and

¾-inch bits is needed. Other tool requirements include bar and C-clamps, as well as standard hand tools. See the comments in Tools and Techniques on page 7.

Building Steps

1. To start, you will cut blanks for the various parts for the rocking horse from 1½-inch stock. If you plan on making this thickness by face-gluing or laminating ¾-inch stock, you will do that next. If not, skip the next paragraph.

From the ¾-inch-thick 1 by 12 lumber, cut 2 each of the blanks calling

for 1½-inch thickness, using the dimensions specified. This includes the pony head, the body, the 4 legs, and the seat. Face-glue each pair together. Use as many C-clamps as necessary to get a good, tight bond along all edges. Use ¾-inch-thick pieces of scrap, approximately 2 inches wide by 10 to 12 inches long, as pads on each side to spread the pressure and prevent the clamps from marring the work. Let each piece dry at least half an hour (depending on the type of glue used) before removing the clamps.

If you are working with solid 2 by 12 lumber, 1½ inches thick, cut out

Cowboys and cowgirls can travel many imaginary miles on the back of this classic rocking pony.

Pony Rocker Pattern on 1" Squares

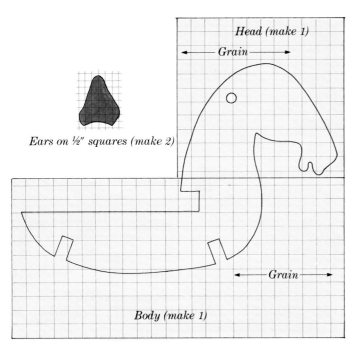

Head (make 1)

← Grain →

Ears on ½" squares (make 2)

Glue line

Body (make 1)

← Grain →

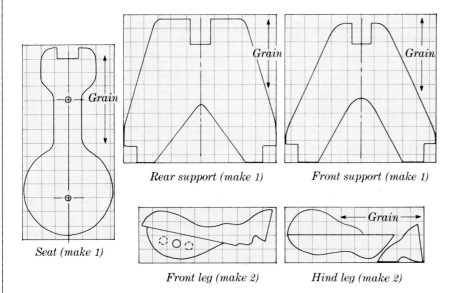

Grain

Rear support (make 1)

Grain

Front support (make 1)

Grain

Seat (make 1)

Front leg (make 2)

Grain

Hind leg (make 2)

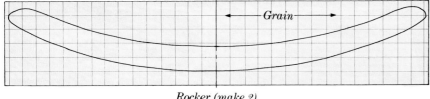

Grain

Rocker (make 2)

the blanks for the pony head, body, legs, and seat to the dimensions given in the materials list. Cut one of each piece.

2. Prepare the pony head-body assembly from the 1½-inch stock. Position the 2 pieces as shown in the illustration. They will be edge-glued together. Check the mating edges; they should be clean and square, with sharp corners. If necessary (and it will be if you laminated the 1½-inch stock), joint the edges using a table saw with a smooth-cut blade, a power jointer, or a hand plane or planer. Glue and clamp, using bar or pipe clamps. If you are an experienced woodworker, you may want to make a doweled or biscuited joint for additional strength. Clean off any excess glue with a damp rag or sponge.

3. After the glue has set, remove the clamps. Transfer the pattern of the head-body piece onto the assembly. See Transferring Shapes From Illustrations on page 13. Saw this out using a band saw or jigsaw with a 2½-inch-long blade. Make this and all the curved cuts that follow carefully. It will mean less sanding later.

4. Transfer the patterns for the front leg and back leg pieces and the seat to the blanks. Saw these out. Note that the seat is notched to fit into the head-body piece. You may want to saw this notch slightly undersized and finish it with a rasp for a snug fit.

5. Mark the location of the handle hole from the illustration, and drill a ¾-inch-diameter hole. Use a backup scrap to prevent the drill from tearing the grain as it emerges on the back side. Be careful to make this hole square and straight. Use a drill press if one is available.

The seat is attached to the body with recessed screws. The screw holes are plugged with dowels, which are sanded flush at the time of assembly. Mark the locations for these 2 screws. Drill blind ½-inch holes, ⅜ inch deep, using a drill stop. Finish drilling the screw pilot holes through the seat, using a 3/16-inch drill bit.

6. The ¾-inch-thick rocker pieces come next. First, saw out the blanks for the 2 supports, transfer the shapes from the scale illustrations, and saw them out. Again, saw the notches slightly undersized and then rasp them out for a good fit with the head and body.

7. You can cut the rockers from solid 1½-inch stock, but the resulting cross grain may make them weak. If you do elect to cut these pieces from solid wood, use a strong hardwood such as oak or hard maple.

The recommended technique is to laminate the rockers from a pair of ¾-inch pieces. Start by transferring the rocker shape onto a piece of cardboard and cutting out the full-sized pattern.

Rip 4 pieces from the ¾-inch lumber, at least 7 inches wide and 32 inches long. You will pair and face-glue these to make two 1½-inch-thick rockers. All the pieces should be free of knots and defects.

The grain on most boards has at least a small amount of angle or slope to it. Play around with the 4 pieces and the rocker pattern to find the 2 pairs that best minimize the cross-grain effect. Do this by positioning the top and bottom boards so that the grain angles are reversed. Then lay out the rocker pattern to take advantage of this. See the illustrations for more details.

8. Face-glue the rocker pairs. Use the gluing and clamping techniques described in step 1. When the glue is dry, remove the clamps, trace the outline of the rocker from the pattern, and saw out the shapes.

9. Sand and smooth all the pieces. Start with a rasp or a stationary belt or disk sander, and round and smooth all the sawn shapes.

The top edges of the seat need to be well rounded. Do this either with a rasp or with coarse sandpaper. If you have a router, you may want to use it for this, with a ³/₁₆-inch or ¼-inch round-over bit. In fact, if you prefer the softer lines that rounded edges will give the rocking pony, you can go over all the edges of the pieces with your router. Just be careful not to round the edges of the notches and the outsides of the supports where 2 pieces are joined.

Sand all saw marks, round the edges, and smooth all the surfaces. Progress from medium-grit sandpaper to fine-grit sandpaper.

10. Set the entire pony up on a workbench or on sawhorses to check for fit. Rasp or sand the bottoms of the 4 legs so that they match the curve of the rockers. Make any other adjustment to the pieces as needed.

11. While the pony is loosely assembled, note that the body will have to be firmly attached to the 2 supports. The best method is to use 2 metal angle brackets for each and then glue to strengthen the joint further. You need to bend the angle brackets to fit the different angles at which the front and back supports meet the body. Put them in a vise and carefully bend them until they fit.

Pony Rocker Assembly

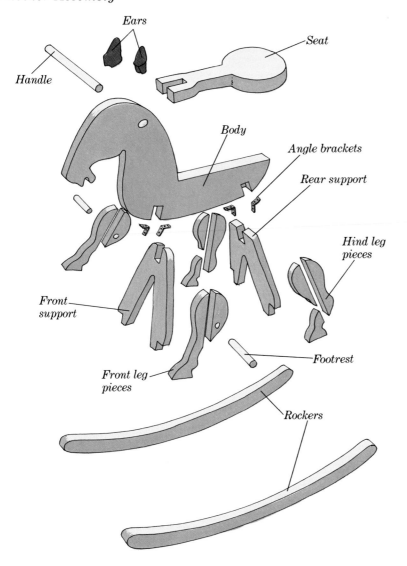

Ears

Handle

Seat

Body

Angle brackets

Rear support

Hind leg pieces

Front support

Front leg pieces

Footrest

Rockers

12. Begin the assembly by attaching the front and back leg pieces to the supports. Position them carefully, following the illustrations. Use glue and the 2-inch finishing nails. When driving the nails home, use a nail set, and countersink the heads about ⅛ inch. Be careful not to mar the surfaces with your hammer. Clean off any excess glue.

13. Now attach the front and back leg-and-support assemblies to the body-head assembly. Apply glue and slip the joints together. Clamp the pieces together with a strap clamp before screwing the angle brackets into place.

14. The rockers are attached to the supports with glue and screws. First check for fit and, using a rasp, make any needed correction to the various parts. Carefully mark the locations of the screws on the bottoms of the rockers. Using the drill, bore blind ½-inch holes, ⅜ inch deep, at each screw location. Use a drill stop to control the depth. Finish drilling through the rockers with a ³/₁₆-inch bit. Hold the rockers firmly in position and extend the screw pilot holes into the supports, using a ⅛-inch bit.

Attach the rockers to the bottoms of the leg-and-support assemblies, using glue and four 2-inch #8 flat-head screws. Plug the screw holes with the ⅜-inch-long pieces of ½-inch dowel, gluing them in place.

15. The seat already has the screw holes prepared. However, you still need to set it in position and extend the screw pilot holes into the body, using a ⅛-inch drill bit. Then apply glue and screw the seat tightly in position, using 2-inch screws. Plug the screw holes with the short dowel pieces, gluing them in place.

16. Cut a ¾-inch dowel to a length of 7½ inches for the handle, and cut two ½-inch dowels, 5½ inches long, for the footrests. Round both ends of the handle and one end of the 2 footrests. The handle hole is already drilled. Insert and glue the handle dowel in place. Drive a 2-inch nail through the head and into the handle to help hold it in place.

The footrest locations will depend on the leg length of the rider. If possible, place the child on the Pony Rocker and position the footrests for his or her leg length. See the illustration for a general idea of the location. Carefully drill horizontal ½-inch holes through the front legs. Apply glue to the dowels and insert them in the holes. The dowels should just emerge on the inside of the legs.

17. Countersink any remaining nails. Fill all these holes with wood filler. When dry, sand flush. At the same time, sand all the screw-hole dowel plugs and the insides of the

footrest dowels flush. Give the entire Pony Rocker a final finish sanding. Dust it off well.

18. Decide whether to paint the pony or give it a natural finish. Spray paint or varnish is easiest. Apply it where there is plenty of ventilation, and read the instructions carefully. At least 2 coats are needed; 3 look even better. You will probably need at least two 12-ounce cans if you use a spray finish.

19. Cut the ears from scrap leather or heavy fabric. Roll them diagonally and tack them in place using the wire brads.

Materials List

The Pony Rocker in the photograph was built out of soft pine because it is light and easy to work. Other even-textured softwoods, such as spruce, have the same features. The rocking horse looks especially attractive in a hardwood such as hard maple, oak, cherry, or alder, with a natural finish.

Because the 1½-inch-thick rocker pieces have cross grain, they are built of two pieces of ¾-inch wood, laminated together, for strength. If you prefer to saw the rockers from single pieces of 1½-inch stock, use a strong wood such as oak or maple.

Most of the pieces of this project are cut out of 2 by 12 lumber, 1½ inches thick. This may be hard to find at a lumberyard in a desirable species. An alternative is to face-glue ¾-inch stock from two pieces of 1 by 12. See Wood Materials, page 11.

If you use 2 by 12 stock, you need approximately 8 feet. An additional 8 feet of 1 by 12 is required. If you plan to build the entire Pony Rocker from ¾-inch lumber, you need approximately 26 lineal feet. The raw material should be of good grade with relatively few knots or other defects. Try to cut the pieces out of clear sections, free of knots. The dowels should be hardwood.

Lumber

Piece	No. of Pieces	Thickness	Width	Length
Front and rear supports	2	¾"	10¾"	11"
Rockers	4	¾"	6"	30½"
Head	1	1½"	11¼"	12"
Body	1	1½"	11¼"	24"
Legs	4	1½"	4"	10"
Seat	1	1½"	6¾"	14"
Footrests	2	½" dowel	5½"	
Screw-hole plugs	7	½" dowel	⅜"	
Handle	1	¾" dowel	7½"	

Hardware and Miscellaneous

Item	Quantity	Size	Description
Leather scraps	1	3" × 8"	For the ears
Nails	20	2"	Bright, finishing
Wire brads	6	1"	Headed
Screws	6	2" × #8–10	Flat head, plated
Angle brackets	4	1½" × 1½"	Flat, plated, with screws
Wood filler	1 tube or small can		Matching wood color
Glue	1 bottle		Woodworking
Sandpaper	2–3 sheets	100–150 grit	Medium and fine
Finish	2 cans		Enamel or clear

ROCKING DINOSAUR

Leaping lizards and great horny toads, it's a rocking dinosaur! Your one- to five-year-old will be the talk of the neighborhood with this friendly version of Tyrannosaurus rex. *Made from 1-inch lumber with simple cuts, this is an easy weekend project.*

Almost all the pieces in this Rocking Dinosaur design are curved shapes, so it is best to use a band saw. However, you could use a hand-held jigsaw if a band saw is not available. A drill equipped with ⅛-inch, ³/₃₂-inch, and ¾-inch bits is needed. Other tool requirements include bar and C-clamps (at least four) as well as standard hand tools. See comments in Tools and Techniques on page 7.

Building Steps

1. Carefully study the illustrations so that you fully understand the construction, especially the sandwiching of the different pieces. Begin the project by cutting out the blanks for all the parts. Cut all but the rockers from clear sections of 1 by 12 pine lumber. Cut the rockers from hardwood. The pine pieces include the main body, the seat, the 2 outer heads, the inner and outer hind legs, the front legs, and the inner and outer tail. Cut the blanks to the dimensions given in the materials list.

2. Enlarge the different shapes from the illustrations and transfer them to the wood blanks. See Transferring Shapes From Illustrations on page 13. Begin with the main body, the seat, and the inner tail piece. Use a jigsaw or a band saw for cutting all these curved shapes. Draw and saw the shapes carefully to save sanding later on.

3. Note that the front legs, the outer hind legs, the inner hind legs, the outer heads, and the outer tails are all pairs that have identical shapes. Stack and temporarily join these paired blanks together. See Duplicate Sawing or Drilling on page 9 for ideas on how to do this. Use the inner tail piece and the head of the body piece, already sawn, as patterns. This will ensure that the shapes match as closely as possible. Note from the illustrations that there are teeth in the mouth of the body (inner) head but not in the outer heads, and that the

large (lower) end of the outer tail pieces extends beyond the end of the inner tail. Saw out all the shapes. Take care to follow the lines closely. Separate the pieces when done.

4. The last curved shapes to be cut are the 2 rocker pieces. Lay out the designs on the 2 pieces of 5-inch by 3-foot hardwood stock. Note the radii shown on the illustrations. You may want to draw out a pattern for the rockers on a piece of cardboard, using a pencil tied to a string and a tack. Then you can transfer the full-sized shape to the wood blanks.

If there is any curve to the grain, try to orient the rocker patterns so that they follow, rather than cross, this curve, minimizing the cross grain and capturing all the strength there is in the pieces. You can double up the blanks for these 2 pieces for sawing. Cut out the rocker pieces.

5. Cut out the 3 rocker supports. These are the only square-cut pieces

Straight out of the prehistoric era, this Tyrannosaurus rex *makes a surprisingly friendly playmate for the rocking set.*

Dinosaur Pattern on 1" Squares

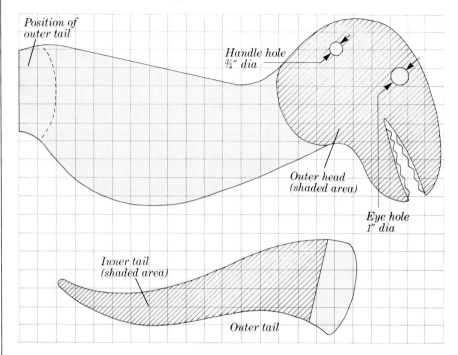

Position of outer tail

Handle hole ¾" dia

Outer head (shaded area)

Eye hole 1" dia

Inner tail (shaded area)

Outer tail

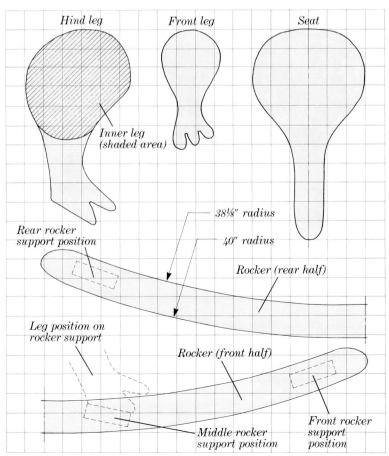

Hind leg

Front leg

Seat

Inner leg (shaded area)

Rear rocker support position

38⅛" radius

40" radius

Rocker (rear half)

Leg position on rocker support

Rocker (front half)

Middle rocker support position

Front rocker support position

in the project and are best sawn on a radial arm or table saw, if available. If you still have some hardwood left, use it for these. It will help strengthen the undercarriage of the rocker.

6. Cut the handle and the footrest to length from ¾-inch dowel stock. Don't cut the eye at this time.

7. Give all the pieces that are to be faced-glued a once-over with a sanding block or pad sander, using medium-grit sandpaper. This prepares the surfaces for gluing. Dust them off thoroughly.

Take another look at the details of the tail assembly in the illustrations. The thickness of the tail end of the main body and of the inner tail piece should be identical. Check this. If they are not, sand one piece or the other until they are.

8. As you assemble the dinosaur, you will be using screws at a number of points. Use flat-head screws, which can be countersunk flush. These screws will be visible even if painted over. If you wish, you can sink each screw head below the surface into a predrilled hole, plug the hole with a wood plug or dowel piece, and then sand it flush. If you elect to do this, start by drilling a ½-inch hole about ¼ inch deep for the plug.

Another alternative is to recess the head of the screw and fill the hole with wood filler. The filler tends to shrink, however, leaving a dimple. To avoid this, fill the hole, allow fill to dry, and fill again if needed.

Plugged or not, all the screws need pilot holes. Use the right size commercial pilot bit, or drill a ³⁄₁₆-inch hole for the upper part of the screw and a ⅛-inch hole for the lower part, and countersink the opening.

9. Start the assembly by aligning carefully and then gluing and clamping an inner hind leg piece to an outer hind leg piece. Remember, there is a left and right assembly. Use wood pads under the clamps to spread the pressure and prevent

Dinosaur Assembly

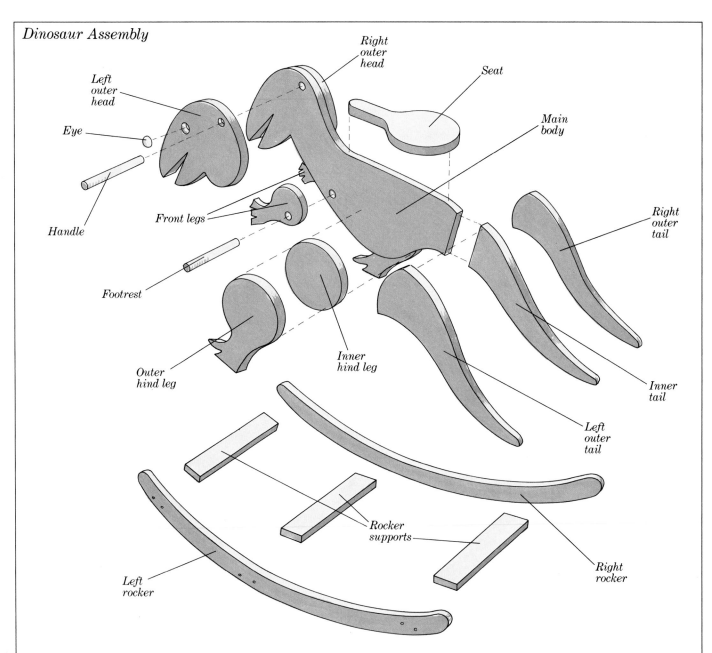

clamp mars. Use enough clamps so that all the edges are tight. Wipe off any excess glue with a damp rag. Allow the glue to dry thoroughly before removing the clamps.

10. Carefully position, glue, and clamp the 2 head pieces on the sides of the head of the main body.

11. Position, glue, and clamp the 2 outer tail pieces to the inner tail, forming a sandwich with the shorter inner tail in the center.

12. Slide the tail assembly into the correct position on the rear end of the body assembly. Glue and clamp.

13. Holding the assembled pieces in a padded vise, smooth the edges with a wood rasp and a power sander. You can also do this with a stationary belt sander. When done, the laminated edges should look like one piece.

Sand all the pieces, including the front legs, the seat, the rockers, and the rocker supports. Sand off saw

marks, round the edges, and smooth the surfaces. Progress from medium-grit sandpaper to fine-grit sandpaper. You can round the edges of the seat with a router fitted with a ³/₁₆-inch or ¼-inch round-over bit.

14. Lay the dinosaur body assembly on its side and drill the ¾-inch hole for the handle through the top of the head. (Refer to the illustrations for the hole locations.) Drill blind

1-inch holes, ¾ inch deep, in each side of the head for the eyes. Take care to drill both these holes straight and square. Use a drill press, if one is available. Do not drill the hole for the footrest at this time. When the entire dinosaur is complete you can position the footrest for the rider.

15. Rasp or sand the ends of the previously cut handle dowel so that they are round. Slip the handle in the hole. Sand it if it is too tight. Apply a small amount of glue in the hole, and tap the handle in place, centering it carefully. Wipe off any excess glue.

16. For the eyes, use a short piece of 1-inch-diameter dowel. Holding it in a padded vise, completely round each end. Saw off ½ inch of each of these rounded ends to make 2 half-spheres. Insert these into the 2 eye holes and glue in place, as shown in the illustrations.

17. Position the rockers and the supports as shown in the illustrations, and drill the screw pilot holes. Use two 1½-inch flat-head screws for each joint. Apply glue, and screw the assembly tight.

18. Attach the hind legs to the body. To position them correctly, dry-clamp them in their approximate position on the body sides. Place the body assembly on the rockers, and adjust the leg positions so that the feet are flat on the center rocker support and the tail is flat on the rear rocker support. When all is correct, lightly mark the leg position on the body.

Before removing the clamps, mark the screw locations and drill pilot holes for the 2-inch flat-head screws. Remove the clamps. Apply glue, align the screw holes, and screw the 2 hind legs tight in their correct position on the sides of the body.

19. While the glue is drying, position, glue, and clamp the front legs to the front sides of the body.

20. When the glue is dry, attach the dinosaur-body assembly to the rocker assembly. Position it correctly and drill pilot holes for 1½-inch screws, 2 each into the bottom of each leg and the tail. Apply glue and screw them down tight.

21. Position the seat, drill pilot holes for the 1½-inch screws, apply glue, and screw in place. You might want to consider plugging these 3 screws. If you decide to do so, you need to drill a blind ½-inch hole before drilling each pilot hole. See step 8.

22. Be sure all the glue joints are dry, and then sit your rider on the seat and determine the proper position of the footrest. Tall children may not require a footrest; they can place their feet on the rockers. Carefully drill a straight and square ¾-inch

hole through the front legs and body. Round the ends of the footrest dowel, apply glue to the center, and insert the dowel through the body, centering it carefully.

23. Give the entire dinosaur a final finish sanding. Give special attention to all areas near glue joints, where glue may have smeared (it will show through clear finish if not sanded off). Dust it off well.

24. Decide whether to paint the dinosaur or give it a natural finish. Either looks good. Spray paint goes on easily and is easy to clean up, so it is the recommended method. Apply it where there is plenty of ventilation, and read the instructions carefully. At least 2 coats will be needed. Three look even better. You will probably need at least two 12-ounce cans, if spray finish is used.

Materials List

Soft pine, including ponderosa and white pine, is a good selection for this project. It is easy to work and light in weight. You could also use other even-textured softwoods or hardwoods. A 12-foot piece of 1 by 12 should be sufficient if the boards are reasonably clear. All the parts should be cut from clear sections that are free of knots and other defects.

The rocker pieces, when sawn, will have some cross grain. To reduce the chance of these pieces breaking, it is recommended that you make them from a strong hardwood, such as oak or maple. You will need 2 pieces approximately 5 inches wide and 3 feet long. The dowels should be hardwood. See Wood Materials, page 11.

Lumber

Piece	No. of Pieces	Thickness	Width	Length
Main body	1	¾"	11½"	23"
Seat	1	¾"	6"	11"
Outer heads	2	¾"	8"	10½"
Inner hind legs	2	¾"	5½"	6"
Outer hind legs	2	¾"	5½"	10½"
Front legs	2	¾"	3"	9"
Inner tail	1	¾"	4"	15"
Outer tails	2	¾"	5"	16"
Rockers	2	¾"	5"	36"
Rocker supports	3	¾"	2¼"	10½"
Handle	1	¾" dowel		9"
Footrest (optional)	1	¾" dowel		7"
Eye	1	1" dowel		1"
Screw hole plugs (optional)	30	½" dowel		¼"

Hardware and Miscellaneous

Item	Quantity	Size	Description
Screws	24	1½" × #8	Flat head, plated
Screws	6	2" × #8	Flat head, plated
Wood filler	1 tube or small can		Matching wood color
Glue	1 bottle		Woodworking
Sandpaper	2–3 sheets	100–150 grit	Medium and fine
Finish	2–4 cans		Enamel or clear

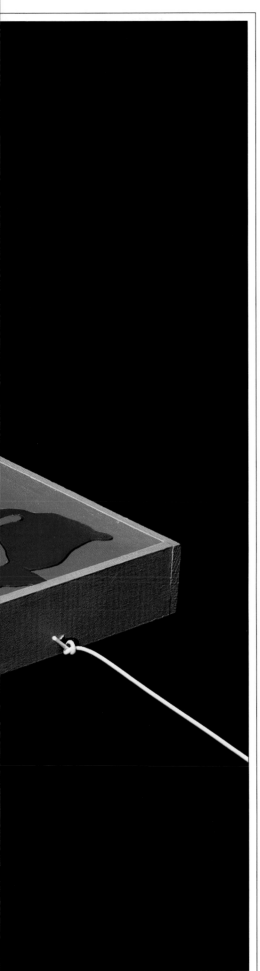

GAMES AND DOLL TOYS

Designed to test the skills of all ages, the games in this chapter are fairly simple to make. The Puzzle Wagon will fascinate one- to three-year-olds. The other games—the Nine-Block Puzzle and the Ring Toss Game—are for children ages five and up, as well as adults. For youngsters they are fun and entertaining, and for more mature and competitive players they can present a real challenge.

A book on children's wooden toys would not be complete without the classic doll toys. The Doll Cradle, Dollhouse, and Dollhouse Furnishings are all charming and lend themselves to the builder's personal touch. These toys, especially the dollhouse and furnishings, are good projects to have your children work on with you. The creativity sparked by decorating a dollhouse is great to watch and leads to hours and hours of fun.

This Puzzle Wagon doubles as a game and a pull toy. The puzzle pieces can be geometric shapes, the letters of a child's name, numbers, or whatever the builder chooses. See page 86.

NINE-BLOCK PUZZLE

This puzzle takes 47 moves to complete. It will probably be too frustrating for children under eight and can even confound adults. The problem is to move the large block from the upper right corner of the board to the upper left corner. This should keep anyone, child or adult, occupied for a while. The game has its roots in early American history and was sometimes called the piano game or dad's puzzle. It can be made in a single afternoon.

For best results, use a radial arm or table saw to make the straight, square cuts and to rip the side pieces for this project. If done carefully, a handsaw can certainly do the job. A flap sander in an electric hand drill makes smoothing the blocks easier. See the comments in Tools and Techniques on page 7.

Building Steps

1. Cut the puzzle-box bottom to size. Make sure the saw is cutting square, and use a fine-tooth blade to keep the edge from splitting.

Puzzle Pattern

Cut blocks from 1" (¾"-thick) stock.

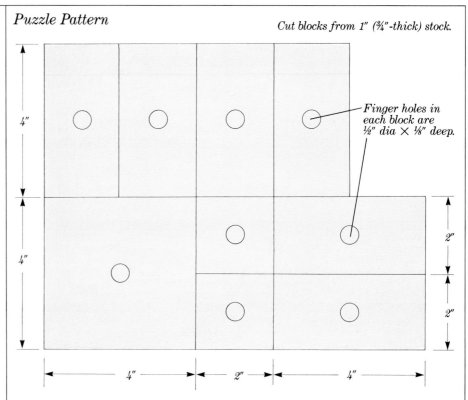

Finger holes in each block are ½" dia × ⅛" deep.

This attractive and deceptively simple-looking puzzle will take even the most skillful player a long time to complete.

2. Rip the side and end pieces from the ¾-inch lumber. Since these are ½ inch thick by 1 inch wide, you need to rip the 1-inch widths first and then rerip to a ½-inch thickness. Be careful when ripping these narrow pieces. Keep the blade down as low as possible and use a push stick and hold-downs. Cut to length.

Note: The sides of the puzzle box shown here were butt-joined. The dimensions given are for that type of corner. You may want to get fancier and miter the corners. In that case, adjust the lengths accordingly.

3. Before you assemble the puzzle box, give the top surface of the plywood box bottom a thorough sanding. Assemble the sides and bottom as shown. Use glue, and tack the sides in place with the brads. If you prefer not to use the brads, you must clamp the sides in place.

4. Saw out the small, medium, and large blocks to the correct dimensions. Saw them accurately, and check that they fit snugly in the box but still move easily.

5. To drill a shallow finger hole in the center of each block, first lightly draw diagonal lines from the corners to locate the center of each block. If you are using a drill press (the preferred tool), you may want to clamp a back fence on the table to make it easier to locate the hole on all but the large block. Experiment on a piece of scrap with different drill speeds to get the cleanest holes. A higher speed will probably work best. Use a conventional split-point drill bit with sloping shoulders, not a brad-pointed bit. A ½-inch-diameter bit was used for the project pictured, but you could also make a larger hole. The holes are only ⅛ inch deep, so adjust the stop accordingly. Drill all 9 shallow holes.

6. Sand the blocks, smoothing all the surfaces and rounding the corners slightly. A stationary belt sander is the best tool for this, if one is available. A flap sander on a hand-held drill works well to sand out and smooth the finger holes.

Check to see if any internal voids are showing on the plywood edges of the puzzle box. Also, if you used finishing brads to hold the sides in place, you might want to countersink them. Fill any of these holes with filler. After the filler is dry, sand it flush. Continue sanding the box. Progress from medium-grit to fine-grit sandpaper. Sand off all saw marks from the sides, and round them slightly. When done, clean off all the sanding dust.

7. If you used hardwoods, you can give the board a natural finish, using clear gloss or semigloss. Lacquer works well because it dries fast, doesn't build up too thickly, and looks especially bright. Spray paint also works well. Be sure to give all the pieces 2 or 3 coats. Sand between coats with a very fine (400+ grit) no-load sandpaper.

Puzzle Assembly

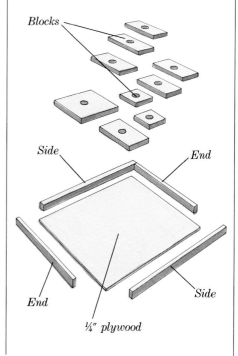

Blocks

Side

End

End

Side

¼" plywood

Materials List

The puzzle-box bottom is made from ¼-inch plywood. You can use a piece of AC-grade softwood plywood or, if desired, plywood faced with birch or some other hardwood. This makes an attractive finished board. A piece 8 by 11 inches, final size, is needed.

You can make the blocks from any ¾-inch-thick wood of your choice. Pine is fine, but again, a hardwood such as walnut, cherry, or hard maple with a natural finish looks great. The border strips are also made from ¾-inch-thick stock. A piece 5½ inches wide by 4 feet long should be more than enough for all the parts needed. Try to cut all the pieces from clear sections of the lumber. See Wood Materials, page 11.

Lumber

Piece	No. of Pieces	Thickness	Width	Length
Puzzle-box bottom	1	¼" plywood	8"	11"
Small blocks	2	¾"	2"	2"
Medium blocks	6	¾"	2"	4"
Large block	1	¾"	4"	4"
Sides	2	½"	1"	11"
Ends	2	½"	1"	8"

Hardware and Miscellaneous

Item	Quantity	Size	Description
Wire brads	20	⅝"	Bright, finishing
Wood filler	1 tube or small can		Matching bottom wood color
Glue	1 small bottle		Woodworking
Sandpaper	2 sheets	100–150 grit	Medium and fine
Finish	1 can		Clear lacquer

PUZZLE WAGON

*A*s both a puzzle and a toy to tow, this wagon will entertain children from one to three years of age. Feel free to create your own designs for the puzzle part of the wagon. You can customize the shapes using your child's initials or name, the shape of a favorite pet, geometric shapes, or anything else that strikes your fancy.

This is a fun project for someone with a new (or old or borrowed) scroll saw. In lieu of that, a coping saw can be used to cut out the puzzle pieces. A table saw or radial arm saw is useful, but not mandatory, for cutting out the straight and square-shaped pieces. You also need a drill with ⅛-inch, ⁵/₁₆-inch, and ½-inch bits and four C-clamps. If you elect to make your own wheels, a hole saw or circle cutter is helpful. See the comments in Tools and Techniques on page 7.

Building Steps

1. Cut out the plywood parts, including the ¼-inch-thick bottom and the ¾-inch-thick puzzle board. Be sure the cuts are square and that the pieces are identical in their dimensions. Use a plywood or smooth-cut cabinet blade to keep the edge from splitting.

2. Cut out the wagon sides and ends. These were sawn from ¾-inch stock and then ripped to the ¼-inch thickness. See Cutting Thin Stock on page 8 for some options and techniques for creating thin stock. One-quarter-inch plywood or thicker solid wood will also work.

Puzzle Wagon Assembly

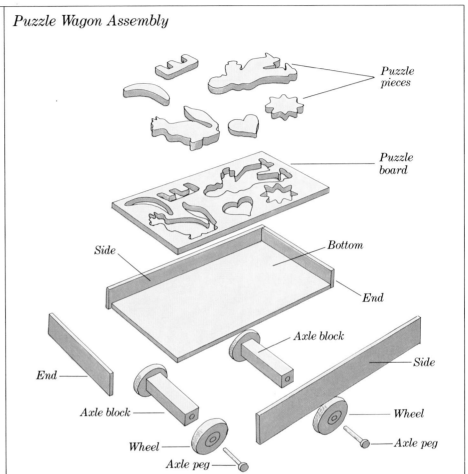

Puzzle pieces

Puzzle board

Side

Bottom

End

Axle block

End

Side

Axle block

Wheel

Wheel

Axle peg

Axle peg

Toddlers will delight in the shapes and colors of this toy as well as in the challenge of putting all the pieces back.

3. Saw the 2 axle blocks from a scrap of ¾-inch lumber.

4. Sand the flat faces of all the pieces to remove any saw marks and to smooth the surfaces.

5. Trace the puzzle designs from the illustrations onto the ¾-inch plywood puzzle board (or draw shapes of your choice). See Transferring Shapes From Illustrations on page 13.

6. You need to drill a small saw-blade entrance hole in each shape to insert the coping or scroll saw blade. Experiment with a piece of scrap to find the smallest hole that will work for the blade you will be using. Drill the holes in an inside corner or some other unobtrusive spot in each design.

Using a coping or scroll saw, very carefully cut out the shapes. If you mis-saw any of the puzzle shapes, you can recut it from a piece of scrap ¾-inch plywood.

7. Sand the edges of both the puzzle board and the puzzle pieces. Round the corners so that there are no sharp edges. Check for fit. The pieces should fit loosely enough that little fingers can remove them easily.

If there are any voids in the plywood edges, fill these with wood filler. When dry, sand the filler flush.

8. Start the assembly by gluing the puzzle board to the wagon bottom. Use woodworking glue and C-clamps. Place blocks between the clamps and the piece to spread the pressure and to keep the clamps from marring the wood. Wipe away any excess glue.

9. Attach the sides and ends as shown in the illustrations, using the ¾-inch brads and glue.

10. Drill ¼-inch holes through the axle blocks. Be sure that these holes are straight and square.

11. If you have elected to make your own wheels, cut them out now from ¾-inch material. You can use a 2-inch hole saw or a circle cutter (with a ¼-inch center bit). Use the circle cutter only in a drill press.

If you make your own wheels, you can use 2 pieces of ¼-inch dowel, 5 inches long, for the axles. You will want to rebore the holes in the axle blocks to ⁵/₁₆ inch.

Materials List

Plywood, both ¼ inch and ¾ inch thick, is a principal material for this project. You need to use a good grade: AC-grade softwood plywood or Baltic birch or another hardwood plywood.

The project shown used ¼-inch solid pine for the wagon sides and ends, ripped on a table saw from ¾-inch stock. If you are unable to do this and are not able to find any lumber ¼ inch thick, you can substitute plywood or thicker wood. Any attractive wood can be used. See Wood Materials, page 11, and Cutting Thin Stock, page 8.

Lumber

Piece	No. of Pieces	Thickness	Width	Length
Wagon bottom	1	¼" plywood	5½"	11"
Puzzle board	1	¾" plywood	5½"	11"
Wagon sides	2	¼"	1⅜"	11⅜"
Wagon ends	2	¼"	1⅜"	5½"
Axle blocks	2	¾"	1½"	3"

Hardware and Miscellaneous

Item	Quantity	Size	Description
Wheels	4	½" × 2"	With ¼" axle holes
Axle pegs	4	¼" × 1⅜"	
Wire brads	20	¾"	Finishing
Screw eye	1	Small	
Plastic cord	1	36"	
Wood filler	1 tube or small can		Matching wood color
Glue	1 small bottle		Woodworking
Sandpaper	2 sheets	100–150 grit	Medium and fine
Finish	1 can		Enamel or clear

12. Glue the 2 axle blocks to the bottom of the wagon, positioning them as shown in the illustrations. Clamp the pieces until the glue has dried.

13. Sand away all machine marks, round all the corners and edges, and smooth all the surfaces.

14. Attach the wheels. If you are using turned wheels and axle pegs, slide the wheels onto the pegs and then glue them in place in the axle blocks. If you made your own wheels and axles, slide the axles through the blocks and glue the wheels on.

15. If the wood is attractive, you can give the wagon a natural finish. Otherwise, a bright gloss enamel looks attractive. Spray finish is recommended, either clear or colored. Be sure to follow the instructions on the can and spray in a well-ventilated place, away from any source of ignition. Give the project at least 2 coats of finish.

16. Attach the screw eye in the center front of the wagon. Tie on the pull cord.

Puzzle Wagon Pattern on ½" Squares

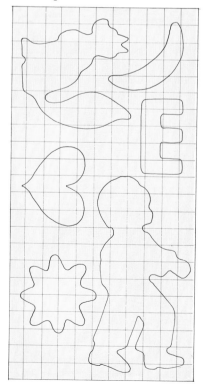

RING TOSS GAME

On the surface this looks like an easy ring toss game. However, it is very challenging. The object is to toss a ring over one of the pegs at the top or middle of the board but to avoid landing on one of the pegs at the bottom.

Children just about any age can play but, realistically, this game is best played by those ages five and up. The rules are very simple: You score 25 points for landing on one of the top three pegs, 50 points for landing on one of the two pegs below, and 100 points for landing on the one big peg. If you should miss and your ring lands on the bottom pegs, you lose 25 points. The score is totaled and the winner declared after each player has had 10 turns with the three rings.

You can build this project with hand-held tools, but a table or radial arm saw helps a lot in getting all the cuts square and straight. These saws also make ripping and fitting the edges easier. You need a coping saw, jigsaw, or scroll saw to cut the rings. Other tools required include a drill with ⅜-inch, ½-inch, and ¾-inch bits. A 1¼-inch bit, hole saw, or circle cutter would simplify the cutting of the holes in the rings, but you can do this with a coping or scroll saw. See the comments in Tools and Techniques on page 7.

Building Steps

1. Cut the game board to size. Make sure the saw is cutting square.

2. Check the illustrations carefully for the locations of the peg holes. Note that there are three ½-inch holes near the top of the board, two ¾-inch holes approximately 4 inches below those, and one 1¼-inch hole centered

4 inches below the ¾-inch holes, to form a triangle. Five ⅜-inch holes are located approximately 2¼ inches below the bottom of the 1¼-inch peg hole. Carefully locate all these holes on the board. Use an awl to indent the center of each hole location. This will help keep the drill in position and prevent it from running.

3. Place the game board firmly on a piece of scrap wood to help keep the holes from splitting out when the drill bit emerges. Drill all the holes. Use brad-pointed bits if possible; they cut a cleaner hole, especially in plywood. Use a drill press if you have one.

You may not have a 1¼-inch bit. An alternative is to saw this hole out with a coping or scroll saw and finish it to the exact size with a rat-tail rasp. Another option is to not make a hole at all, but to screw the 1¼-inch peg to the board. The screw, of course, will come through the back and into the dowel. Use a fairly long screw, at least 1½ inches, along with glue.

4. Cut the dowel pegs to length. Saw the correct number of pegs from the various dowel diameters to the lengths specified in the materials list. Sand all of the dowels, rounding one end of each. Be careful not to sand the square ends too much, or they will fit loosely in the holes.

5. You have a number of choices for edging. You can simply glue thin ¾-inch by ¾-inch strips to the edges of the game board, using butt joints at the corners. You can also cut a ¼-inch rabbet in each strip for the plywood and join the corners with a 45-degree miter cut. This is what was done for the project pictured. The strips have an overall length of 15¾ inches. If you choose this alternative, you may want to make the edging strip a little wider than ¾ inch.

Another option is to use picture-frame molding. You can either make this yourself or purchase it. Use mitered corners. If you elect to use the ¾-inch edging, rip and, if desired, rabbet the edge strips. If you are mitering the corners, set the miter gauge or saw to 45 degrees and carefully saw the lengths to fit.

Here is a game the whole family can play together. It is simple to construct and a lot safer than darts.

6. Glue the edging pieces to the edges of the board, using the ½-inch brads to hold them in place. When the glue is dry, give the board and edges a good sanding. Remove all saw marks, round the edges, and smooth the surfaces.

7. Next, glue the dowels in place. If you are screwing the 1¼-inch peg to the board, drill a ³/₁₆-inch pilot hole through the board. Countersink the hole on the back side. Drill a ⅛-inch pilot hole into the center of the peg. Apply glue and screw peg in place.

8. Cut a strip of ¾-inch stock for the tilt board. Lightly sand it, and attach it to the bottom of the board back with brads and glue. This gives the game board a slight tilt when attached to the wall.

9. Cut the 3 rings from the ⅛-inch hardboard. First, cut the 3 blanks. The most efficient way to saw the rings is to temporarily stack them for sawing. Refer to Duplicate Sawing or Drilling on page 9 for ideas on temporarily tacking pieces together. Draw the 2 circles, one 4 inches in diameter, the other 1⅞ inches in diameter. Drill a saw-blade entrance hole; saw the inside hole using a coping or scroll saw, then saw the outside circle. Separate the rings and sand them smooth and round the edges.

You can cut the inside holes somewhat larger if you want to make the game easier. You might want to make several sets of rings with different-sized center cutouts. This will help suit different skill levels.

10. If you use hardwood plywood, a natural finish looks good. Use a clear gloss or semigloss finish. Lacquer works well: It dries fast, doesn't build up too thickly, and looks especially bright. Spray finish is recommended, either clear or colored. Give the board 2 or 3 coats. You may decide to paint the rings a bright, distinctive color.

11. The last thing to consider is hanging the game board. You can hang it like a picture, using screw eyes, wire, and a picture hanger. Or you can mount it more permanently by screwing it into the wall.

Ring Toss Assembly

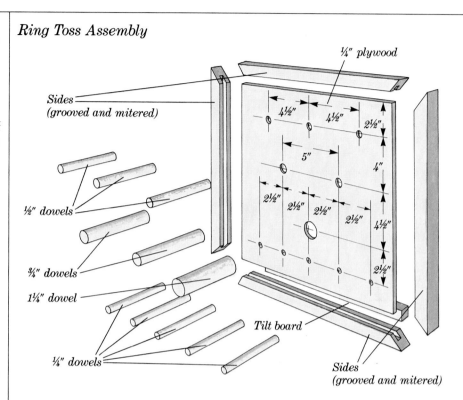

Materials List

The game board is cut from a piece of ¼-inch plywood. Birch or other hardwood plywood looks best, but AC-grade softwood plywood will work fine. A 15- by 15-inch piece, final size, is needed. The rings are made from ⅛-inch-thick board; tempered hardboard is the best choice. You can use ¼-inch plywood, but the rings will be heavier. A 5- by 14-inch piece should be more than enough. See Wood Materials, page 11.

You can edge the board with strips cut from scrap pieces of ¾-inch stock. An attractive hardwood looks best, especially if birch or other hardwood plywood is used for the board. An alternative is to use picture-frame stock. This molding can usually be purchased locally in a variety of shapes and sizes, or you can make it yourself. Approximately 7 lineal feet of the strips or molding are needed.

You need less than 10 lineal inches of each type of dowel, except for the ⅜-inch dowel, of which you need a total of 14 inches. All dowels should be hardwood.

Lumber

Piece	No. of Pieces	Thickness	Width	Length
Rings	4	⅛" hardboard	4¼"	4¼"
Game board	1	¼" plywood	15"	15"
Edges or molding	4	¾"	¾"	15¾"
Tilt board	1	¾"	¾"	13"
Ring pegs	5	⅜" dowel	2½"	
Ring pegs	3	½" dowel	3"	
Ring pegs	2	¾" dowel	3"	
Ring peg	1	1¼" dowel	3"	

Hardware and Miscellaneous

Item	Quantity	Size	Description
Wire brads	20	½"	Bright, finishing
Glue	1 small bottle		Woodworking
Sandpaper	2 sheets	100–150 grit	Medium and fine
Finish	1 can		Enamel or clear
Picture hanger, wire, and 2 small screw eyes for hanging the game			

DOLL CRADLE

This Doll Cradle is an easy afternoon workshop project. It is more than 10 inches wide and 20 inches long and will handle most of the standard doll sizes. It can accommodate the cat or puppy, too, although your two- to five-year-old is likely to be the only one having fun.

Although there are alternatives, a table saw is the preferred tool to rip the ½-inch stock and cut the dado grooves. A jigsaw or band saw facilitates the cutting of the curved rockers, and a drill press is useful for boring the dowel holes. Other tools needed include basic hand tools, a drill with a ¼-inch bit, and bar and C-clamps for the assembly. See the comments in Tools and Techniques on page 7.

Building Steps

1. Cut out the pieces for the cradle box. Cut the bottom from the ¼-inch plywood, making sure it is perfectly square. Saw out the 2 end pieces and the 2 side pieces from the ¾-inch solid wood stock.

2. Machine the 2 side pieces and end pieces down to ½-inch thickness. Review Cutting Thin Stock on page 8. As is discussed in that section, you have several options. One is to surface the pieces to ½-inch thicknesses with a planer. Another is to rip the pieces on edge at a band or table saw, using a smooth-cut rip blade, and then jointing, planing, or sanding to smooth the sawn face. If you do the resizing on a table saw or band saw, take special care. Use a push stick, and watch your fingers while doing the ripping.

3. Cut a ¼-inch by ¼-inch dado slot in the end and side pieces, ½ inch from the edge, as shown in the illustrations. The plywood bottom should fit snugly in these slots. If available, use a dado blade in a table saw for making these cuts. Otherwise, you can cut them with 2 passes of the saw. Another alternative is to cut the dadoes with a router fitted with a ¼-inch straight bit.

4. Draw out the curved shapes on the upper part of the side pieces, and saw out with a jigsaw or band saw. You can clamp the 2 pieces and saw them together, or you can tack them together temporarily, using techniques discussed in Duplicate Sawing or Drilling on page 9.

5. Put together the cradle-box pieces on a workbench and check for fit. Give the flat surfaces of the pieces a good sanding. Use a

hand-held or stationary power sander, if available. Start with medium-grit sandpaper and then move to fine-grit sandpaper. Be careful not to round the edges or corners (or thin the edges of the plywood) at this time.

6. Assemble the cradle box, using glue and the 1-inch brads. Clamp in both directions, using bar or pipe clamps. Use clamp pads to prevent marring. Carefully wipe off any excess glue with a damp rag or sponge.

7. While the cradle box is drying, go back to the saw and cut out the 2 headboard and footboard tops and the square blanks for the headboard and footboard rockers. Cut these from 1 by 4 stock.

8. Drill the holes for the headboard and footboard dowels. Clamp the side edges of the headboard rocker blank and headboard top together.

A soft, fuzzy blanket is all that is needed to make this cradle the perfect spot for a doll-sized snooze.

As an alternative to clamping, you can tack them together temporarily.

Consult the illustration and mark the locations of the dowel holes. Drill down through the rocker blank and into, but not through, the top piece. Use a drill stop to control this. The resulting blind holes in the top should be ½ inch deep. A drill press is the best tool for this job. If you are drilling by hand, be sure the holes are straight and square.

Do the same thing with the footboard rocker blank and top piece.

9. Note from the illustrations the ¼-inch by ¾-inch rabbet cut in the flat side of the 2 rocker pieces. Make this cut. Use a dado blade, or cut the rabbet with 2 rip passes of the saw. A router can also be used.

10. Cut the final rocker shapes: Draw the shapes on the rocker pieces, using a drawing compass, if

you like. The outside curve has an 8-inch radius, and the inside curve has a 7-inch radius. Be sure to position the rabbet cuts on the top.

Now cut the outside shape, using a jigsaw or band saw. You can join these 2 pieces temporarily and saw them together. The inside cut can also be gang-sawn at the same time.

To make the inside cut, you need to drill a saw-blade entrance hole in the cutout area. Then use a hand coping saw, a jigsaw, or a scroll saw to cut the inside piece out. With the coping or scroll saw, you need to detach the blade, insert it through the hole, reattach the blade, and saw.

11. Measure and cut the 14 dowels for the headboard and the footboard. These are from ¼-inch hardwood dowels.

12. Carefully sand the headboard and footboard rockers and tops,

giving special attention to the inside cutout of the rockers. Sand off all the saw marks, round the edges, and smooth the surfaces. Progress from medium- to fine-grit sandpaper. Sand the dowels lightly. They should fit snugly, but not tightly, in the ¼-inch holes in the headboard and footboard pieces.

13. Check the illustration to see how the headboard and footboard parts go together. Lightly apply glue and tap the dowels into the blind holes in the top pieces. Be careful here—if the dowels fit too tightly or too much glue is used, hydraulic pressure can develop and the piece can split. Wipe off any excess glue with a damp rag or sponge.

Apply glue to the ends of the dowels and slide them through the rocker pieces, tapping gently. Keep doing this until the rocker is 5 inches from

Cradle Pattern on ½" Squares

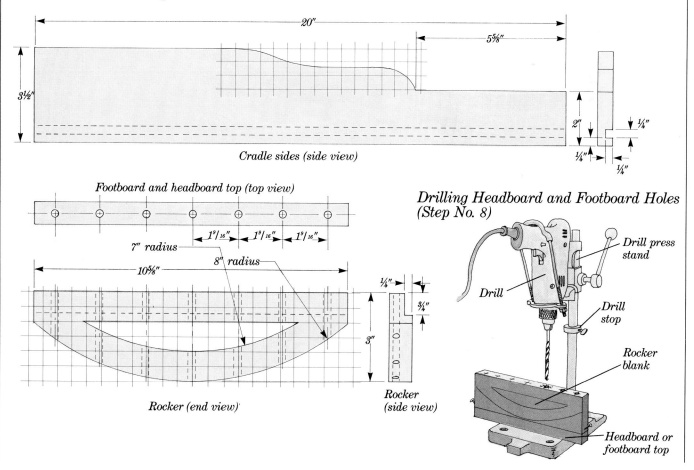

Cradle sides (side view)

Footboard and headboard top (top view)

7" radius

8" radius

10⅝"

Rocker (end view)

Rocker (side view)

Drilling Headboard and Footboard Holes (Step No. 8)

Drill press stand

Drill

Drill stop

Rocker blank

Headboard or footboard top

Cradle Assembly

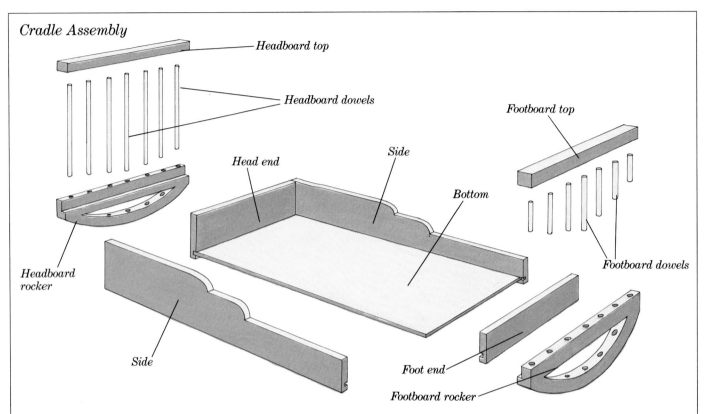

Headboard top

Headboard dowels

Footboard top

Side

Head end

Bottom

Footboard dowels

Headboard rocker

Side

Foot end

Footboard rocker

the top piece on the headboard and 1⅜ inches from the top piece on the footboard. The dowel ends will stick out. You can saw these off and sand them flush after the glue has dried. Again, wipe off any excess glue.

14. Countersink the nails in the cradle box, and fill them with wood filler. When dry, sand flush. Give the entire box a thorough sanding, rounding the edges and corners.

15. Attach the rocker assemblies to the completed bed. Use the brads and glue for this. Wipe off excess glue when done.

Sand the entire cradle a final time, then dust it off well.

16. If you have used an attractive wood and prefer a natural finish, a clear satin polyurethane varnish or lacquer looks attractive. If you do this, you may want to add some color trim or decoration. Use spray finish, whether you use clear or color, for easy application and cleanup. Be sure to read the instructions on the can carefully. Give all parts at least 2 coats of paint.

Materials List

The project shown was built with soft pine because it is light and easy to work. However, this cradle would look quite attractive in a hardwood such as hard maple, oak, cherry, or alder with a natural finish. A piece of 1 by 4 lumber, approximately 10 feet long, or the hardwood equivalent, is required. All the pieces should be cut from clear sections of the lumber.

The cradle bottom is cut from a 1- by 2-feet piece of ¼-inch Baltic birch plywood. You can also use AC-grade softwood plywood. Approximately 9 lineal feet of ¼-inch hardwood dowel is needed. See Wood Materials, page 11.

Lumber

Piece	No. of Pieces	Thickness	Width	Length
Bottom	1	¼" plywood	10"	19⅜"
Foot end	1	½"	2"	9⅝"
Head end	1	½"	3½"	9⅝"
Sides	2	½"	3½"	20"
Headboard and footboard tops	2	¾"	¾"	10⅝"
Headboard and footboard rockers	2	¾"	3"	10⅝"
Headboard dowels	7	¼" dowel		8½"
Footboard dowels	7	¼" dowel		5"

Hardware and Miscellaneous

Item	Quantity	Size	Description
Wire brads	20	1"	Finishing
Wood filler	1 tube or small can		Matching wood color
Glue	1 small bottle		Woodworking
Sandpaper	2 sheets	100–150 grit	Medium and fine
Finish	1 can		Enamel or clear

DOLLHOUSE

This is worth every minute spent on its construction. Your children will play with it for hours and hours and remember it for the rest of their lives. It's designed for the three- to eight-year-old, but don't be surprised if you find older and younger children playing with it.

A table saw or radial arm saw is a must for building this dollhouse. Along with the saw, you need a wobble dado or dado blade set, and a plywood cutting blade. A band saw is needed to cut the shingles. Other tools required include a saber saw, jigsaw, coping saw, or scroll saw; a drill with ⅛-inch and ½-inch bits; a staple gun; a hot-melt glue gun; and other standard hand tools. Both C-clamps and bar or pipe clamps are needed in the assembly. See the comments in Tools and Techniques on page 7.

Building Steps

1. To get a good fit and end up with an attractive dollhouse, you must saw all the pieces squarely and accurately. Before you start, it might be a good idea to check out the performance of the saw you'll be using. If you are using a table saw, read the manual and check that the fence is parallel with the saw, that the saw-to-fence ripping-width distance gauge is reading accurately, that the saw-tilt zero stop is an accurate 90 degrees, and that the miter gauge can be set to cut a true square or right angle. Make any adjustment needed. Make the same types of checks and adjustments if you are using a radial arm saw. Install a plywood-cutting blade

Children love to help build projects like this Dollhouse. Once it is complete, there's the fun of furnishing and landscaping the estate.

or your smoothest cabinet blade to minimize grain splitout on the plywood edges.

2. Lay out all the ⅜-inch plywood pieces on a sheet of plywood to get the most efficient use of the material. Lightly identify each piece with a pencil. Rough-saw these with a hand-held saw to a manageable size. Then cut the 2 side walls, the front wall, the attic floor, the second-story floor, the front and back roof, and the main floor of the dollhouse to final dimensions on the table or radial arm saw. Use the dimensions shown in the materials list.

3. Do the same with the required pieces from the ¼-inch plywood. This includes the 2 second-floor partitions and the first-floor partition.

4. Finish cutting the basic house parts by sawing out the 2 gable ends from the 1 by 6 pine. Set the miter gauge or saw to the required 40-degree roof slope or angle.

5. Next, mount a ⅜-inch-wide dado cutter on your saw, setting it to cut ⅛ inch deep. Test the cut on some scraps; the ⅜-inch plywood should fit in it snugly. Cut the horizontal dado grooves in the front and side pieces. These will hold the second-story floor.

6. Readjust or set the dado to a ¼-inch width. Test with some scraps of the ¼-inch plywood. Note that some of the ¼-inch dado grooves for the partitions are cut all the way across, whereas others are blind dadoes, stopping part of the way across the piece and having a square end.

Dollhouse Floor, Front Wall, and Partition Patterns

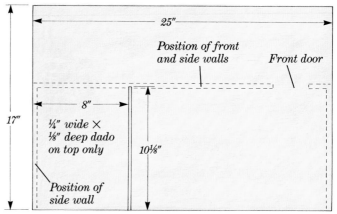

Main floor (⅜" stock)

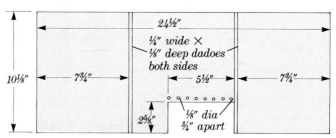

Second-story floor (⅜" stock)

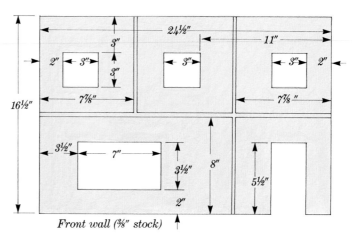

Front wall (⅜" stock)

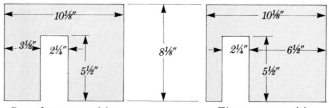

Second-story partition (make 2)   *First-story partition*

Dollhouse Floor, Gable, and Side Wall Patterns

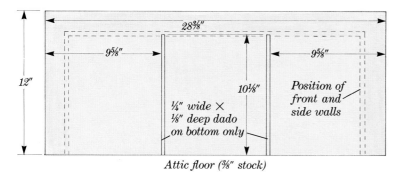

28⅜"

9⅝"   9⅝"

12"

10⅛"

¼" wide ×
⅛" deep dado
on bottom only

Position of
front and
side walls

Attic floor (⅜" stock)

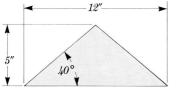

12"

5"

40°

Gable (make 2 on ¾" stock)

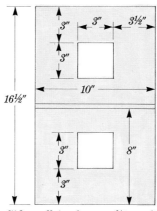

3"   3"   3½"

3"

10"

16½"

3"

8"

3"

Side wall (make 2 on ⅜" stock)

Staircase Assembly

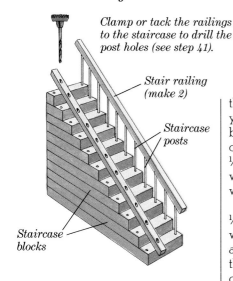

Clamp or tack the railings
to the staircase to drill the
post holes (see step 41).

Stair railing
(make 2)

Staircase
posts

Staircase
blocks

There are two ways to handle a blind dado cut. One is to stop the cut near the end of the groove and finish up the square end with a chisel. This is difficult to do with a table saw, since you cannot see where the blade is. However, you can draw reference marks on the piece and the saw table or fence and stop cutting when you reach the mark.

The other way to make this cut, and the recommended method, is to cut the dado groove entirely across

the piece or go a short distance beyond the stopping point. Then come back and fill in the unneeded portion of the groove, either with a ⅛-inch by ¼-inch wood strip that you glue in or with wood filler. Sand either flush when dry.

Choose a method and cut the ¼-inch partition grooves in the front wall, in both sides of the second floor, and in the attic and main floors. Cut the grooves ⅛ inch deep. Finish the grooves, making sure to stop them at the correct places.

7. Draw the window and door openings in the ⅜-inch-thick front and side walls. Drill a ¼-inch saw-blade entrance hole inside these openings, and saw each one out with a coping, saber, or scroll saw. Make the cuts as carefully and as smoothly as possible.

Do the same with the second-story floor, sawing out the cutout for the stairway entrance. Next, cut out the door opening in each of the 3 partition pieces.

8. Set the dollhouse parts together and see if they all fit. You may need someone to help you with this. Make any necessary adjustments.

9. As you can see from the illustrations, ⅛-inch railing-post holes are needed along one side of the stairway opening in the second-story floor. Once the dollhouse is assembled, you won't be able to get a drill into the space to make these holes, so now is the time to do it.

To locate these holes correctly in relation to the railing, you need to drill the holes through both at the same time. This means you have to stop and saw out the railing stock.

10. Put the saw blade back on the saw and rip about 3 lineal feet of ⅜-inch-square railing stock from the cedar or redwood 1-by stock. Take care in sawing these small pieces, and watch your fingers. Use a push stick and hold-downs. Cut the landing railing piece to length, saving the rest of the railing stock for later.

Clamp the railing piece in the correct position but on the underside of the second-story floor. Locate the 8 holes from the illustrations. Using a ⅛-inch drill with a stop or a drill press, drill down through the floor and ³⁄₁₆ inch deep into the railing. Be careful not to go all the way through.

11. All the pieces need a good sanding at this point. Sand the flat surfaces smooth, progressing from medium- to fine-grit sandpaper. Sand the edges of all the cutouts smooth, removing the saw marks and sharp corners.

12. Follow along with the illustrations as you begin to put the pieces of the dollhouse together. Work at a reasonable pace so that the glue has not set when all pieces are in place.

Begin by gluing and nailing the sides and front together, using woodworking glue and the ⅝-inch finishing brads. Wipe off any excess glue from this and all subsequent glue joints with a damp sponge or rag.

13. Insert the second-story floor into the dado grooves in the front and side walls, and glue and nail in place.

14. Position the attic floor so that there is a 1½-inch overhang on the front and sides. Glue and nail in place. Position the main floor, and fasten it in place.

15. Slide the 3 room partitions into their correct dado grooves, and glue and nail them in place.

16. Pull all the pieces together tightly with bar or pipe clamps. Let the assembly dry for several hours.

17. Cut out the siding. Rip the siding pieces to the required dimensions from the ¾-inch-thick 1 by 6 pine stock. You need approximately 60 lineal feet. Use the table saw, or you can use a band saw for a rough-sawn appearance. The band saw is probably the easier and safer of the 2 tools for this.

Sawing these very thin pieces, ⅛ inch thick, is going to require some special techniques, such as hold-downs and a push stick, and should be attempted only by someone experienced with a power saw. As an alternative, you can often purchase sheets of thin wood material, such as balsa wood, at a hobby shop and cut the strips with a sharp knife. Dollhouse suppliers also carry some of this type of material.

Sand the siding stock, if necessary.

18. Cut the siding strips to length as you go for the sides and front, stopping and starting around the doors and windows. Start to apply the siding, using glue and ¼-inch staples in a staple gun. You can use hot-melt adhesive instead of the woodworking glue and staples, if you like. Start at the bottom and allow a 3/16-inch overlap. If you are using woodworking glue, be sure to wipe off any excess with your damp rag.

If you are stapling, drive the staples in the overlap area so that they do not show. Be careful when stapling near the ends, as the siding may split. Continue to apply the siding until you reach the attic floor line. You may need to rerip or cut the last pieces of siding for a proper fit.

19. For easier assembly, the gables are attached after the siding is in place. Apply the siding to the gables. Trim the ends of the siding with a fine-tooth saw such as a coping saw, or use a sharp knife. A stationary belt sander works well to get the siding ends flush with the gable slopes.

20. Now attach the gables to the house. Use glue and ⅝-inch nails to fasten the bottoms of the gables to the attic floor. Nail and glue the 2 roof pieces in place at the same time.

21. Using a fine file and sandpaper attached to a block, sand the siding smooth and flush around all the window and door openings. Do the same to the outside corners of the dollhouse.

22. The living room walls in the dollhouse are paneled with a scrap of printed wood grain ⅛ inch thick. This is optional. If you choose to add the paneling, cut the material to the correct interior dimensions and attach it with hot-melt adhesive. If you do this to the walls with windows, the width of the trim for the windows must be made thicker to match the thickness of the paneling.

23. Rip the stock for the window and door framing, the molding, and other trim pieces, as shown in the materials list. Cut them to length. All of these pieces are ⅛ inch thick, so the precautions used when sawing siding also apply here. Precut strips and thin sheets from a hobby or dollhouse supplier are a great convenience here.

Sand all these pieces smooth, removing saw marks and lightly rounding the edges.

24. Cut the plastic windowpanes to shape. This can be done with a power saw if a very fine-tooth blade is used. Hold the plastic firmly on the table to prevent chattering.

25. Start with the picture window. Study the illustrations carefully for the details of construction. Cut the pieces of the inner window frame to length, insert them in the window opening, and secure them in place using hot-melt adhesive.

26. When installed, the outside edges of the windowpanes are framed on 4 sides and sandwiched between 2 sets of window moldings to hold them in place. These moldings, in turn, are centered inside the window frame.

To accomplish this, start by gluing one set of moldings—top, bottom, and 2 sides—in place on the inside of the window frame. Use model airplane cement for this. (Hot-melt adhesive is too thick.) You may want to use pins to hold these pieces in place while the glue sets.

27. Tack the windowpane in place against the installed molding, using model airplane cement. Install the other set of molding frames to secure the windowpane in place.

28. Complete the window assembly by adding the top, bottom, and side window-trim pieces to the inside and outside of the house. Either hot-melt adhesive or model airplane cement can be used.

29. Using the same construction methods, complete all the windows.

30. The front door is next. Frame and trim the door as you did the windows.

31. Cut the door to size from the ¾-inch-thick pine and then resaw it to a ½-inch thickness, using a table or band saw. Sand it smooth.

At the same time, cut the door facing and decorations from the cedar or redwood stock.

Dollhouse Assembly

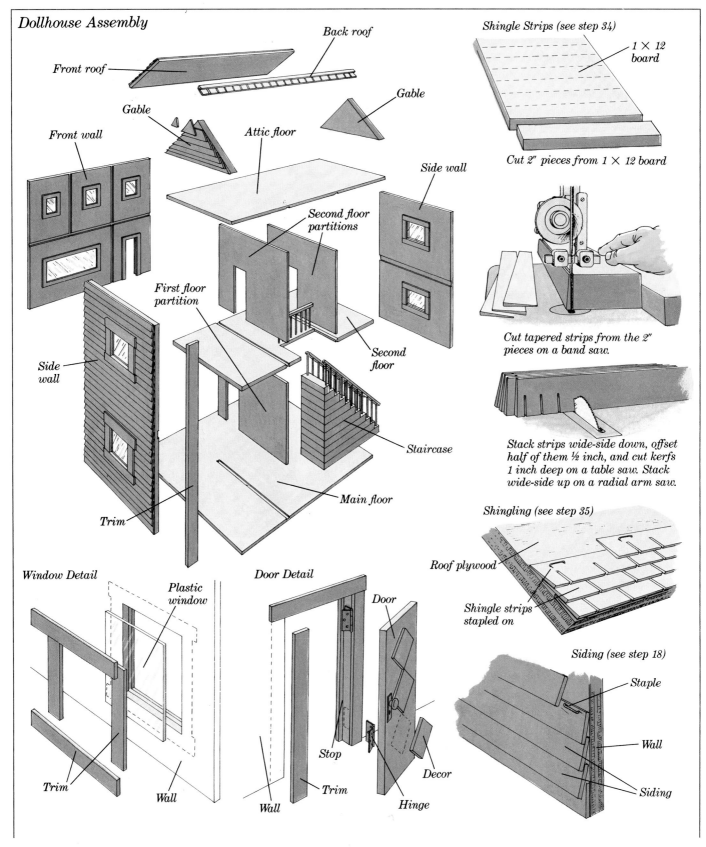

Back roof

Front roof

Gable

Front wall

Gable

Attic floor

Side wall

Second floor partitions

First floor partition

Side wall

Second floor

Staircase

Trim

Main floor

Window Detail

Plastic window

Trim

Wall

Door Detail

Door

Stop

Wall

Trim

Decor

Hinge

Shingle Strips (see step 34)

1 × 12 board

Cut 2" pieces from 1 × 12 board

Cut tapered strips from the 2" pieces on a band saw.

Stack strips wide-side down, offset half of them ½ inch, and cut kerfs 1 inch deep on a table saw. Stack wide-side up on a radial arm saw.

Shingling (see step 35)

Roof plywood

Shingle strips stapled on

Siding (see step 18)

Staple

Wall

Siding

32. Glue the door facing and door decorations in place with model airplane cement. Install the doorknob assembly, using the hardware and instructions in the kit. Attach the hinges.

33. Install the door in the door opening by attaching the hinges to the door frame. Close the door flush with trim and install the stop piece.

34. Start making the shingles. Cross-cut seven or eight 2-inch strips from the 1 by 12 cedar or redwood, using a table or radial arm saw. The grain will be running crosswise. If there is any appreciable cup or warp in the strips, cut them in two.

Now move to the band saw and tilt the table 1 or 2 degrees. You will slice the shingle strips from the 2-inch pieces by sawing them on edge. Set the band saw fence (or clamp a guide) so that the thick edge of the shingle strip will be 3/32 inch thick. Use a resaw blade, 1/2 inch or wider. Be sure to use a push stick to clear the pieces past the blade. Reverse the material on each pass to get the desired taper. Each piece of 3/4-inch stock should yield 6 shingle strips. You need at least 33 strips, each 11 1/4 inches long, or the equivalent.

Install a wood extension fence on the table saw miter gauge if you do not already have one attached. Set the miter gauge to cut 90 degrees. Now stack about a third of the sawn shingle strips, thick side down, offsetting half of them by 1/2 inch. Carefully holding the strips together or, better yet, clamping them, cut a series of 1/8-inch-thick saw kerfs, 1 inch deep and 1 inch apart, to simulate individual shingles. Do the same with the rest of the shingle strips. This machining can also be done on a radial arm saw.

35. Start to lay the shingles. Place a layer of shingle strips along the eaves of the large roof, allowing a 1/4-inch overhang. Double up the first layer. Tack the strips down with staples or hot-melt adhesive. Place the next row or layer on top of the first strip, following the illustrations. Separate the 2 rows by 1 inch. Stagger the kerf

Materials List

Plywood, both 1/4 inch and 3/8 inch, is the principal material for this dollhouse. Use very good AA- or AB-grade softwood plywood that is clear on both faces and relatively free of interior veneer voids. If you cannot find this in softwood plywood, look over the stock of hardwood plywood at a lumberyard. You need approximately 1 foot by 3 feet of 1/4-inch material, and 4 feet by 5 feet of 3/8-inch-thick plywood.

Some solid wood is also required for this project. Most of the trim is 1 by 6 white pine, and the shingles and outside trim are 1 by 12 redwood. You can substitute other soft pines or even-textured woods for the white pine, and cedar can be used instead of redwood. You need approximately 26 lineal feet of the 1 by 6, and 10 feet of 1 by 12. See Wood Materials, page 11.

Lumber

Piece	No. of Pieces	Thickness	Width	Length
Plywood House Parts				
Second-floor partitions	2	1/4″ plywood	8 9/16″	10 1/8″
First-floor partition	1	1/4″ plywood	8 1/8″	10 1/8″
Side walls	2	3/8″ plywood	10″	16 3/4″
Front wall	1	3/8″ plywood	16 3/4″	25″
Attic floor	1	3/8″ plywood	12″	28 3/8″
Second floor	1	3/8″ plywood	10 1/8″	24 1/2″
Front roof	1	3/8″ plywood	9″	28 3/8″
Back roof	1	3/8″ plywood	1 1/2″	28 3/8″
Main floor	1	3/8″ plywood	17″	25″
Siding (from 1 × 6)				
Lap siding for sides	60	1/8″	3/4″	10 1/2″
Lap siding for gables	20	1/8″	3/4″	10 1/2″
Lap siding for front	30	1/8″	3/4″	25″
House Trim (from 1 × 6)				
Trim for front	2	1/8″	3/4″	16 3/4″
Trim for side and rear	6	1/8″	3/4″	17″
Trim for back roof	2	1/8″	1″	6″
Small-Window Trim, Molding, and Framing (from 1 × 6 pine)				
Framing for side	28	1/8″	1/2″	3 1/4″
Framing for top and bottom	28	1/8″	1/2″	2 3/4″
Molding for side	28	1/8″	1/8″	2 3/8″
Molding for top and bottom	28	1/8″	1/8″	2 3/4″
Trim for side	28	1/8″	1/2″	2 3/4″
Trim for top and bottom	28	1/8″	1/2″	3 1/8″
Picture-Window Trim, Molding, and Framing (from 1 × 6 pine)				
Framing for side	4	1/8″	1/2″	3 1/4″
Framing for top and bottom	4	1/8″	1/2″	10 1/4″
Molding for side	4	1/8″	1/8″	3 3/8″
Molding for top and bottom	4	1/8″	1/8″	10″
Trim for side	4	1/8″	1/2″	3 3/4″
Trim for top and bottom	4	1/8″	1/2″	11 1/8″
Door-Frame Trim and Framing (from 1 × 6 pine)				
Framing for side	2	1/8″	1/2″	5 7/8″
Framing for top	1	1/8″	1/2″	2 7/8″
Trim for side	4	1/8″	1/2″	5 7/8″
Trim for top	2	1/8″	1/2″	3 13/16″
Doorstop	1	1/8″	1/8″	5 7/8″
Front door	1	1/2″	2 1/2″	5 3/4″
Door base (second floor)	2	1/8″	1/4″	2 1/2″
Door facing*	1	1/8″	1/2″	5 3/4″
Door decorations*	3	1/8″	1 1/8″	1 1/8″

*From redwood or cedar

Materials List (continued)

Lumber

Piece	No. of Pieces	Thickness	Width	Length
Stairway Parts and Gables (from 1 × 6 pine)				
Staircase block	1	¾″	2½″	8¼″
Staircase block	1	¾″	2½″	7½″
Staircase block	1	¾″	2½″	6¾″
Staircase block	1	¾″	2½″	6″
Staircase block	1	¾″	2½″	5¼″
Staircase block	1	¾″	2½″	4½″
Staircase block	1	¾″	2½″	3¾″
Staircase block	1	¾″	2½″	3″
Staircase block	1	¾″	2½″	2¼″
Staircase block	1	¾″	2½″	1½″
Staircase block	1	¾″	2½″	¾″
Stair railings	2	⅜″	⅜″	11½″
Landing railing	1	⅜″	⅜″	6¼″
Gables	2	¾″	5″	12″
Roof Parts (from 1-by cedar or redwood)				
Shingles	33	⅛″	2″	11¼″
Trim for roof peak	2	⅛″	⅝″	29″
Dowels				
Landing and staircase posts	30	⅛″ dowel		2½″

Hardware and Miscellaneous

Item	Quantity	Size	Description
Clear plastic	7	1⁄16″ × 2¹¹⁄16″ × 2¹¹⁄16″	For windows
Clear plastic	1	1⁄16″ × 3¹¹⁄16″ × 10″	For picture window
Hinges*	2	Very small	For the door
Doorknob assembly*	1	Very small	For the door
Wire brads	50	½″	Finishing
Wire brads	50	⅝″	Finishing
Staples	200–300	¼″	For staple gun
Pins	10		Dressmaking pins
Wood filler	1 tube or small can		Matching wood color
Adhesive	4–6 sticks		Hot melt
Cement	1–2 tubes		Model airplane
Glue	1 small bottle		Woodworking
Sandpaper	2–3 sheets	100–150 grit	Medium and fine
Finish	1 can		Enamel or clear

*From a dollhouse supplier

slots so that each is over the center of the shingle below it. Fasten in place.

Continue to place the shingle strips, working up to the ridge. Cut them to length as you go, or use a sharp knife to trim along the gable ends. When you reach the ridge or peak, you need to trim the last row of shingles to fit. Finish by shingling the opposite roof.

36. Finish the exterior of the doll-house by attaching the remainder of the trim. This includes the roof-peak trim, the front-wall side trim, the side-wall side trim, the rear side trim, and the back-roof trim. Glue these in place using hot-melt adhesive and ½-inch brads when needed.

37. The stairway is built from a stack of ¾-inch-thick blocks, each one ¾ inch shorter than the other. Cut the step parts from ¾-inch pine to the dimensions shown in the ma-terials list. Stack, glue, nail, and clamp these pieces together. When the glue is dry, sand all the surfaces flush and smooth. Slightly round the stairway edges.

Note that the stairway is not perma-nently attached to the dollhouse. This makes it easier for the dollhouse keeper to move furniture, redecorate, or whatever.

38. Cut the 2 staircase railings to length from stock already sawn.

39. From the ⅛-inch dowel stock, cut the posts for the landing and staircase railings to length. You need 30 of these, so it pays to clamp up a stop arrangement to get them all equal in length.

40. Drill vertical ⅛-inch blind holes, ⅛ inch deep, for the railing posts on each edge of the stairway, centered on each step, as shown in the illustrations. Use a stop on the drill bit to control the depth.

41. Blind holes are also needed in the railings. One way to get the an-gles and spacing right is to center each rail above the holes and clamp it onto the staircase. Drill the holes directly above the holes in the stair-case, holding the drill vertical. Use a stop on the drill to control the depth of the holes. Unclamp, and turn the railings upside down and reverse them end-for-end so that the angles are correct.

42. Sand the 2 staircase railings and the landing railing smooth. Round the edges. Glue the dowel posts into the railings and then into the staircase. Follow the same proce-dure for the landing railing, using the holes previously drilled into the second-story floor.

43. Give everything a final sand-ing, smoothing all the rough edges. When done, dust off well.

44. Paint the dollhouse the color or colors of your choice. You might want to use varnish or some other clear finish on the cedar shingle roof and front door. The trim can be painted a complementary color. An acrylic latex enamel works well for the paint.

Many dollhouse keepers wallpaper the interior walls, using an expired wallpaper sample book acquired from a local wallpaper store. Regular wallpaper paste can be used.

DOLLHOUSE FURNISHINGS

*F*urnishing your first house can be a big expense. These miniature versions of furniture don't cost much, and they are easy to make from scraps of lumber and odds and ends.

Using bits of 2 by 4, scrap plywood, some Styrofoam from a packing case, and pieces of fabric, you can stimulate the creativity and world of make-believe for your special little person.

A table saw or radial arm saw is helpful for building these furnishings. Other useful tools include a jigsaw, coping saw, or scroll saw; a drill with $1/32$-inch, $1/8$-inch, $1/4$-inch, and $1/2$-inch bits; a staple gun; a hot-melt glue gun; a model airplane knife; a wood

rasp; and other standard hand tools. Some C-clamps are also needed. See the comments in Tools and Techniques on page 7.

Building Steps

Be sure to use your imagination on these and any other furnishings. Customize them according to materials at hand and use your own innovations.

You are limited only by your imagination when it comes to furnishing a dollhouse.
These basic items are sure to inspire many other furnishing ideas.

Kitchen Sink and Wall Cabinet

1. Saw the pieces for the kitchen sink and the wall cabinet from a block of 2 by 6. Sand these smooth.

2. Saw out the cutout for the sink in the top of the sink cabinet, as shown in the illustrations. You will cover the front and back of this later with the sink enclosure pieces. Saw out the cutout in the base of the wall cabinet. Use a coping saw, scroll saw, jigsaw, or band saw for the 2 cutouts. Sand them smooth.

3. Cut the door and drawer shapes for both cabinets from ⅛-inch stock. Cut the top, base, and sink enclosure pieces for the sink cabinet from the same stock. Drill a ¼-inch saw-blade entrance hole in the top and cut out the hole in the kitchen sink top with a coping saw, scroll saw, or jigsaw. Sand all these parts smooth.

4. If you want to paint the doors and drawers a different color, this is the time to do so.

5. Attach the sink enclosure pieces, the cabinet drawers, the base, and kitchen sink top, using hot-melt adhesive or model airplane cement. Clamp the pieces, if necessary to keep them tight.

6. Drill ⅛-inch holes behind the sink for the faucet and handles. Bend some #8 copper wire to shape, apply glue to the end, and insert it into the center hole for the faucet. The handles are made from four ½-inch lengths of ⅛-inch dowel, glued together as shown in the illustrations. Glue the handles in place with model airplane cement or hot-melt adhesive. A ½-inch washer goes into the bottom of the sink recess for the drain. Hold it in place and fill in around the edges with hot-melt adhesive.

7. Drill 1/32-inch holes in all the locations where drawer knobs and doorknobs are, as shown in the illustrations. Paint the cabinets if you have not already done so. Finally, tack the brass escutcheon pins in place.

Wall Cabinet Assembly

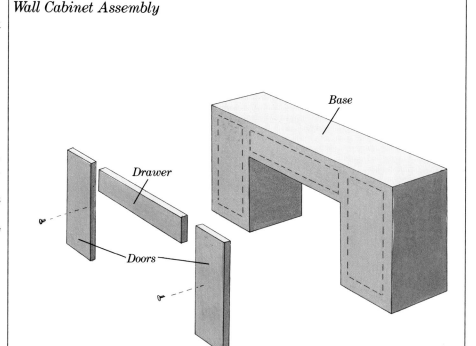

Base

Drawer

Doors

Kitchen Sink Assembly

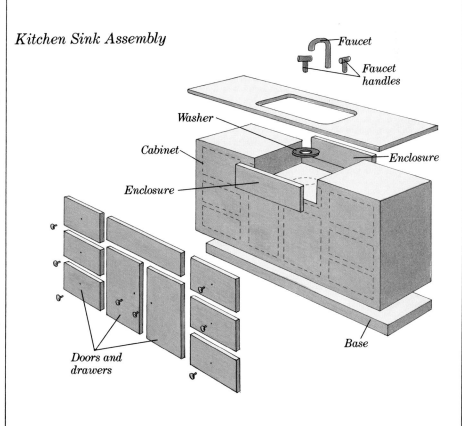

Faucet

Faucet handles

Washer

Cabinet

Enclosure

Enclosure

Base

Doors and drawers

Stool Assembly

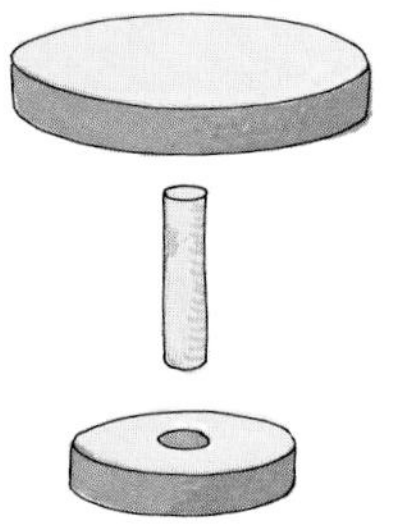

Bench Assembly

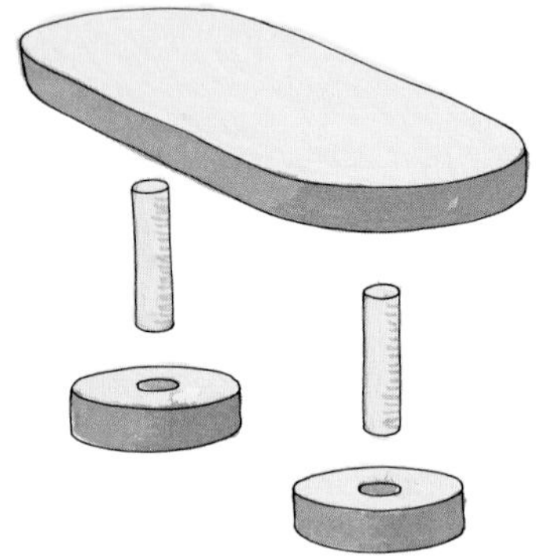

Bench and Stool

1. Draw the shapes of the bench and stool tops on a piece of ⅛-inch stock and the circular bases on a piece of ¼-inch stock. Cut them out.

2. Drill ¼-inch holes in the center of each base piece and in the correct locations in the bench and stool pieces, as shown in the illustrations. Sand all these pieces to round the edges, remove fuzz, and smooth the surfaces.

3. Cut ¼-inch dowels to length for the pedestals. Sand these smooth.

4. Apply glue to the dowels and insert them in place. After the glue has dried, sand to even the dowel ends and surfaces.

5. Paint the furniture the color of your choice.

Materials List

Most of these small items can be built from wood scraps you have around the shop. You need some 1 by 6 and 2 by 6 lumber; some ¼-inch-thick wood; some ⅛-inch plywood; and ⅛-inch, ¼-inch, ½-inch, and ¾-inch dowels. If possible, try to find the right sizes and thicknesses in soft pine or another soft, even-textured wood. You can, of course, face-glue 1 by 6 material to make up the 1½-inch stock. The dowels should be hardwood.

If you have difficulty finding ¼-inch solid wood and ⅛-inch plywood, try a hobby or dollhouse shop. In most cases balsa wood will work fine as a substitute.The Styrofoam pieces are also included in this list. Balsa wood can be used as a substitute for these as well.

Lumber

Piece	*No. of Pieces*	*Thickness*	*Width*	*Length*
⅛-Inch Stock				
Freezer door	1	⅛″	1¼″	2¼″
Refrigerator door	1	⅛″	2¼″	3¾″
Wall cabinet drawer	1	⅛″	¾″	3″
Wall cabinet doors	2	⅛″	1¼″	3″
Kitchen sink drawers	6	⅛″	1″	1¼″
Kitchen sink doors	2	⅛″	1¼″	2¼″
Kitchen sink enclosure	2	⅛″	11/16″	2¼″
Kitchen sink top	1	⅛″	1⅝″	6″
Kitchen sink base	1	⅛″	1¼″	6″
Kitchen sink facing	1	⅛″	¾″	2¾″
Oven door	1	⅛″	2⅞″	2⅞″
Stove drawer	1	⅛″	⅝″	2⅞″
Medicine-cabinet-and-sink back	1	⅛″	4″	8″
Toilet tank lid	1	⅛″	⅞″	2⅜″
Toilet seat cover	1	⅛″	1⅜″	1¾″
Chest upper drawers	2	⅛″	⅝″	1½″
Chest lower drawer	1	⅛″	½″	3⅜″
Chest of drawers top	1	⅛″	1¾″	4¼″
Bureau upper drawers	4	⅛″	⅝″	1½″
Bureau lower drawer	1	⅛″	½″	3⅜″
Bureau top	1	⅛″	1¾″	4¼″
Bureau mirror back strips	2	⅛″	¾″	3½″
Stool tops	2	⅛″	1½″ dia	
Bench top	1	⅛″	1½″	3″
Easy chair backs	2	⅛″	2″	3″
Sofa back	1	⅛″	3″	5″
¼-Inch Stock				
Dining tabletop	1	¼″	4″	4″
Dining table legs	4	¼″	¾″	1″
Dining chair seats	4	¼″	1¼″	1¼″
Bathroom sink base	1	¼″	2⅛″	4″
Bathtub sides	2	¼″	1¾″	5½″
Bathtub bottom	1	¼″	2″	4″
Toilet rim	1	¼″	1⅝″	2⅜″
Stool bases	2	¼″	1″ dia	
Bench bases	2	¼″	¾″ dia	
Bed base	1	¼″	5″	6¾″
Bed footboard	1	¼″	¾″	4 1/16″
Bed headboard	1	¼″	3″	4 1/16″
¾-Inch Stock				
Stove back	1	¾″	3½″	3½″
Bathroom sink top	1	¾″	2½″	4″
Medicine cabinet	1	¾″	1¾″	2½″
Bathtub ends	2	¾″	1¾″	2″
Toilet water tank	1	¾″	1¾″	2⅛″

Materials List (continued)

Lumber

Piece	*No. of Pieces*	*Thickness*	*Width*	*Length*
1½-Inch Stock				
Refrigerator body	1	1½"	2½"	6"
Kitchen sink base	1	1½"	3¼"	6"
Stove body	1	1½"	3½"	3½"
Bathroom sink cabinet	1	1½"	2⅜"	4"
Toilet base	1	1½"	1½"	1½"
Mirror bureau base	1	1½"	2⅞"	3¾"
Chest of drawers base	1	1½"	2⅛"	3⅞"
Wall cabinet base	1	1½"	3¼"	6"
Easy chair bases	2	1½"	2"	2"
Sofa base	1	1½"	2"	5"
Wood Dowels				
Kitchen faucet handles	2	⅛" dowel	½"	
Kitchen sink faucet bases	2	⅛" dowel	½"	
Chair backs/legs	8	⅛" dowel	3⅝"	
Chair front legs	8	⅛" dowel	1¼"	
Chair rungs	12	⅛" dowel	⅞"	
Refrigerator handles	2	¼" dowel	1"	
Stove handles	2	¼" dowel	2⅜"	
Bathroom sink spout	1	¼" dowel	⅞"	
Bathroom sink faucet handles	2	⅛" dowel	½"	
Bathroom sink faucet bases	2	¼" dowel	¼"	
Bathtub spout	1	¼" dowel	⅞"	
Bathtub faucet handles	2	⅛" dowel	½"	
Bathtub faucet bases	2	¼" dowel	¼"	
Bench/stool pedestals	4	¼" dowel	1½"	
Bedposts for head	2	½" dowel	3¼"	
Bedposts for foot	2	½" dowel	2"	
Dining table pedestal	1	¾" dowel	2½"	
Easy chair and sofa arms	6	¾" dowel	2⅛"	
Styrofoam or Balsa Pieces				
Toilet bowl	1	1"	1⅜"	2⅛"
Easy chair back cushions	2	⅝"	2"	2⅝"
Sofa back cushion	1	⅝"	2⅝"	5"
Sofa and chair seat cushions	5	⅝"	1¼"	1½"
Bed mattress	1	½"	5"	5⅞"
Bed pillows	2	1"	1¼"	2⅜"

Hardware and Miscellaneous

Item	*Quantity*	*Size*	*Description*
Fabric		4 sq ft	For bed and chairs
Mirror plastic	1	1¼" × 1½"	For medicine cabinet
Mirror plastic	1	3" × 3¾"	For mirror bureau
Copper wire	1	⅛" × 1½" × #8	For kitchen sink faucet
Brass escutcheon pins	32	½"	Round head
Wire brads	4	½"	Finishing
Washers	1	½" dia	Flat, for drain
Washers	2	1" dia	Flat, for burners
Washers	2	¾" dia	Flat, for burners
Staples	20	¼"	For staple gun
Wood filler	1 tube or small can		Matching wood color
Adhesive	5–6 sticks		Hot melt
Cement	2–3 tubes		Model airplane
Glue	1 small bottle		Woodworking
Sandpaper	2 sheets	100–150 grit	Medium and fine
Finish	1 or more cans or bottles		Model airplane
Paintbrushes	1–2	Small	

Refrigerator Assembly

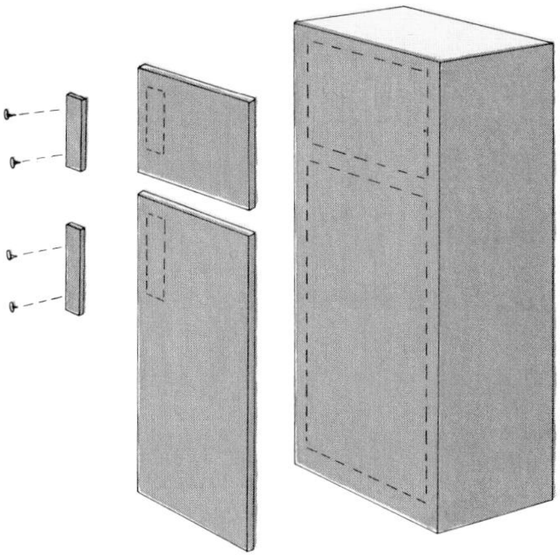

Refrigerator

1. Cut the refrigerator body from a piece of 2 by 6 material to the dimensions specified in the materials list. Use a table saw or whatever you have available.

2. Cut the 2 doors from ⅛-inch plywood or solid wood stock, either using a knife or sawing them to the correct dimensions. If you prefer, you can cut the doors for a side-by-side refrigerator.

3. Sand all the surfaces smooth.

4. Cut a 1-inch length of ¼-inch dowel. Carefully split it in two, lengthwise, and sand the flat split surface smooth. Drill two 1/32-inch holes in each handle for the brass escutcheon pins.

5. If you want to paint the refrigerator body and doors different colors, do so now.

6. Glue the doors and handles to the front of the refrigerator with model airplane cement. Clamp if necessary to keep the assembly tight. Give the piece a final sanding, and paint it if you did not do so earlier.

7. Tap the brass pins into place for the door pulls.

Bathroom Sink and Medicine Cabinet Assembly

Toilet Assembly

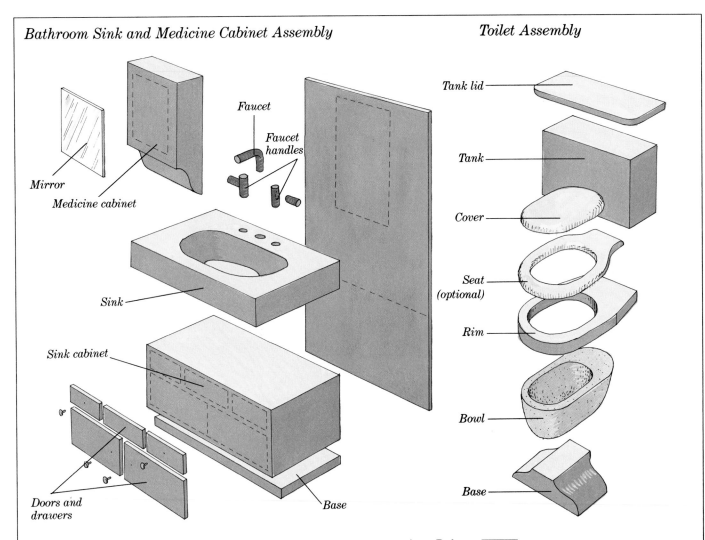

Mirror

Medicine cabinet

Faucet

Faucet handles

Sink

Sink cabinet

Doors and drawers

Base

Tank lid

Tank

Cover

Seat (optional)

Rim

Bowl

Base

Bathroom Sink and Medicine Cabinet

1. Cut out the medicine-cabinet and bathroom sink back from ⅛-inch stock.

2. Cut the bathroom sink cabinet from a piece of 2 by 6. Cut the sink top from a piece of ¾-inch stock. Cut the base from ¼-inch material.

3. Saw the sink bowl in the sink top as shown in the illustrations. Drill a ¼-inch saw-blade entrance hole first, and then saw the cutout with a coping or scroll saw, set at an angle so that the bowl slopes in correctly.

4. Glue all the parts together. Refer to the illustrations as necessary. Use clamps if necessary. Sand all the surfaces flush and smooth after the glue has dried.

5. Cut short lengths of ⅛-inch and ¼-inch dowels for the faucet and handles. Sand the ends round, and glue in place using hot-melt adhesive.

6. Cut the medicine cabinet from ¾-inch material. Shape the bottom with a coping saw, rasp, and sandpaper. Cut a piece of mirror plastic to fit the front, and glue it to the front of the cabinet, using hot-melt adhesive. Glue the sink assembly and the cabinet assembly onto the medicine-cabinet and bathroom sink back.

7. Paint the bathroom sink assembly the color of your choice.

Toilet

1. The toilet is built up from a number of pieces, as shown in the illustrations. Start by drawing the pattern for the base on a piece of 1½-inch stock. Saw this out with a coping or scroll saw, and sand it smooth.

2. Cut the water tank from ¾-inch wood, the rim from ¼-inch stock, and the tank lid and seat cover from ⅛-inch stock.

Toilet Pattern on ¼" Squares

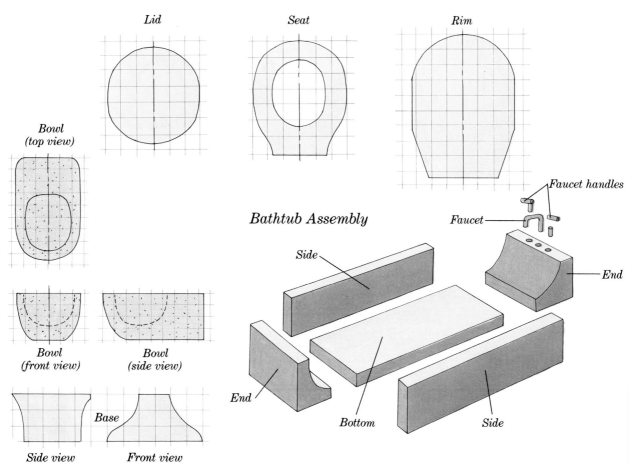

Lid

Seat

Rim

*Bowl
(top view)*

Bathtub Assembly

Faucet handles

Faucet

Side

End

End

Bottom

Side

*Bowl
(front view)*

*Bowl
(side view)*

Side view

Base

Front view

3. The toilet bowl can be made from a piece of 1-inch Styrofoam, or you can use a piece of balsa wood or pine if you prefer. Shape it with a rasp and sandpaper. If you have a rotary rasp, you can hollow out the inside of the bowl.

4. Sand all the pieces smooth, and round the corners. Glue the pieces together with hot-melt adhesive. If you really feel creative, you can shape a toilet seat and hinge it and the cover to the rim.

5. Finish the piece by painting it.

Bathtub

1. You might prefer to make some of the parts for the bathtub from scraps of balsa wood, if you have any around. It is easier to carve and shape than pine.

2. Draw the shape of the bathtub ends on ¾-inch-thick stock, and cut to shape. Cut the bottom and sides from ¼-inch stock.

3. Glue the pieces together, using model airplane cement. Sand all the corners and edges round.

4. Add fixtures as you did to the bathroom sink.

5. Paint the bathtub, giving it 2 or 3 coats.

Bathtub ends (side view)

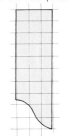

Pattern on ¼" squares (make 2)

Medicine cabinet (side view)

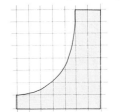

Pattern on ¼" squares

Stove Assembly

Dining Table Assembly

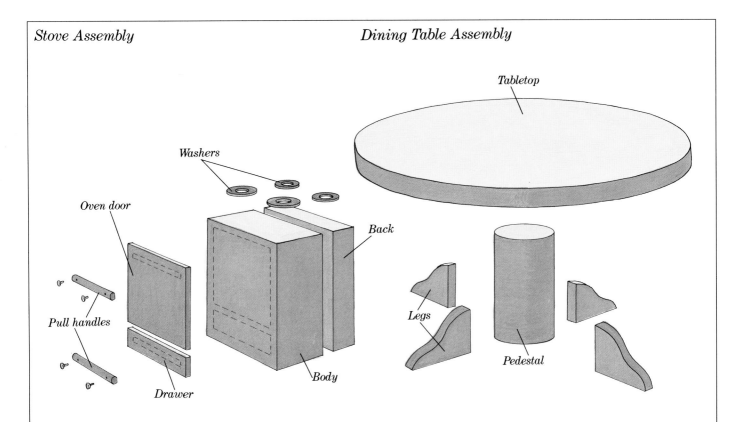

Tabletop

Washers

Oven door

Back

Pull handles

Legs

Pedestal

Body

Drawer

Stove

1. Cut the stove body from 2 by 6 material. Saw the back of the stove body from 1 by 6 stock. Glue these 2 pieces together with woodworking glue, and sand flush when dry.

2. Cut the oven door and drawer front from the ⅛-inch stock. Glue these in place with model airplane cement on the front of the stove, clamping if necessary.

3. Saw two 2⅜-inch pieces of ¼-inch dowel for the pull handles. Sand one side of each dowel flat. Carefully drill 2 holes in each near the ends for the pins. Apply a smear of glue, and place as shown in the illustrations.

4. Give the stove a final sanding, and finish in a color of your choice. Use at least 2 coats.

5. Using hot-melt adhesive, glue two 1-inch and two ¾-inch washers on the top of the stove for burners. You may want to paint these washers black before gluing them.

6. Tap the 4 brass escutcheon pins in place.

Dining Table

1. Draw a 4-inch-diameter circle on the ¼-inch wood for the tabletop. Cut this out with a coping or scroll saw. Sand the edges smooth, rounding them slightly.

2. Cut the 4 legs from the same material. If you are using a table saw, you can saw triangles the right size from the corners of a squared piece, cutting at a 45-degree angle. Then saw, rasp, and sand the legs to shape the curved edges. Sand these pieces smooth.

3. Cut a piece of ¾-inch dowel, 2½ inches long, for the table pedestal.

4. Using model airplane cement, glue the legs in place on the pedestal, and then glue the tabletop on top of the pedestal dowel.

5. Paint the table the color of your choice, using at least 2 coats.

Dining Chairs

1. Using a coping or scroll saw, cut the 4 dining chair seats from ¼-inch stock. Sand these smooth, and round the edges and corners.

2. Drill four ⅛-inch holes in each chair seat as shown in the illustrations. Sand away any fuzz.

3. Cut the necessary pieces of ⅛-inch dowel for the front legs, leg-backs, and rungs. Sand these smooth.

4. Apply glue and tap the front legs into their holes. The ends should be flush with the tops of the chair seats. Sand this surface smooth and flush after the legs are in place and dry. Drive the longer leg-backs through the rear holes, making sure the leg portions protrude the same distance as the front legs. Glue the rungs in place using hot-melt adhesive or model airplane cement.

5. Paint the chairs.

Dining Chair Assembly

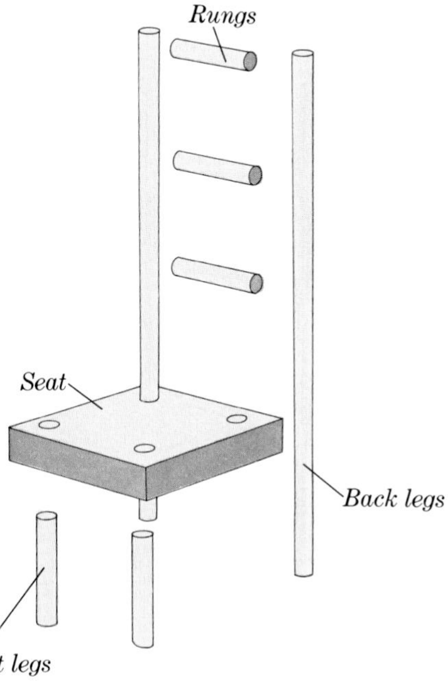

Rungs

Seat

Back legs

Front legs

Bureau Assembly

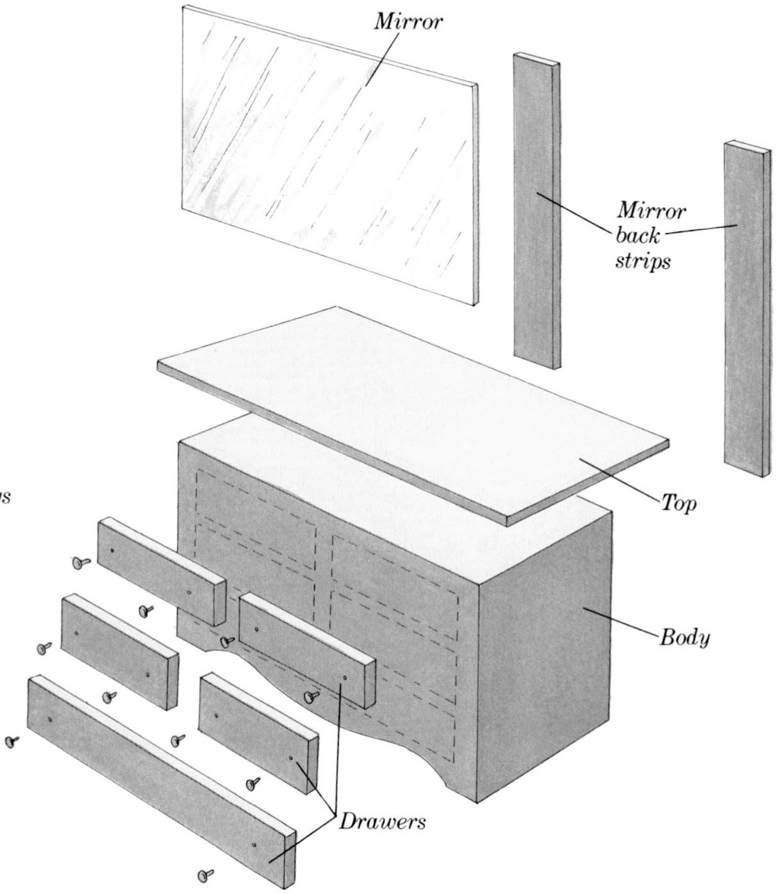

Mirror

Mirror back strips

Top

Body

Drawers

Chest of Drawers Assembly

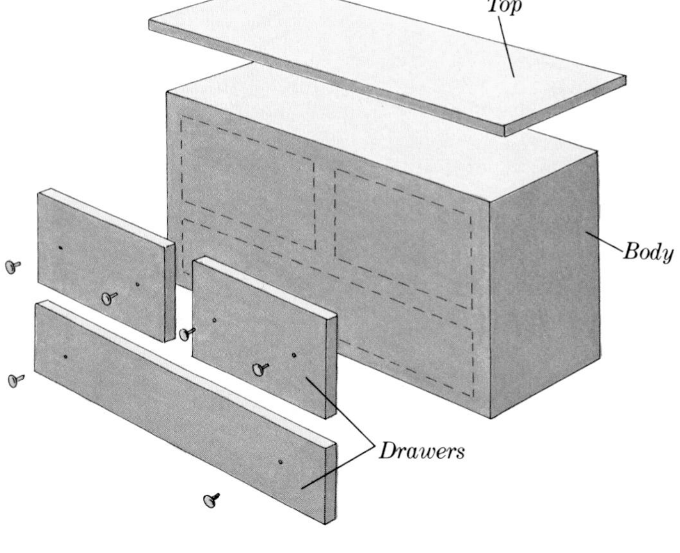

Top

Body

Drawers

Bureau With Mirror and Chest of Drawers

1. Saw the bodies of the mirror bureau and the chest of drawers from 2 by 6 stock. Cut the curved bottom of the bureau with a scroll saw or coping saw.

2. Cut out the tops and the drawer fronts for the 2 items from $\frac{1}{8}$-inch material. Cut the mirror back strips for the bureau from the same stock. After sanding all the pieces, glue them in place, clamping if necessary. Sand the edges of the tops round.

3. Drill $\frac{1}{32}$-inch holes for the drawer knobs, as shown in the illustrations.

4. Cut a piece of mirror plastic to the correct size, and glue it in place using hot-melt adhesive.

5. Paint or stain the 2 pieces of furniture. Tap the brass pins into their predrilled holes.

Bed Base Pattern

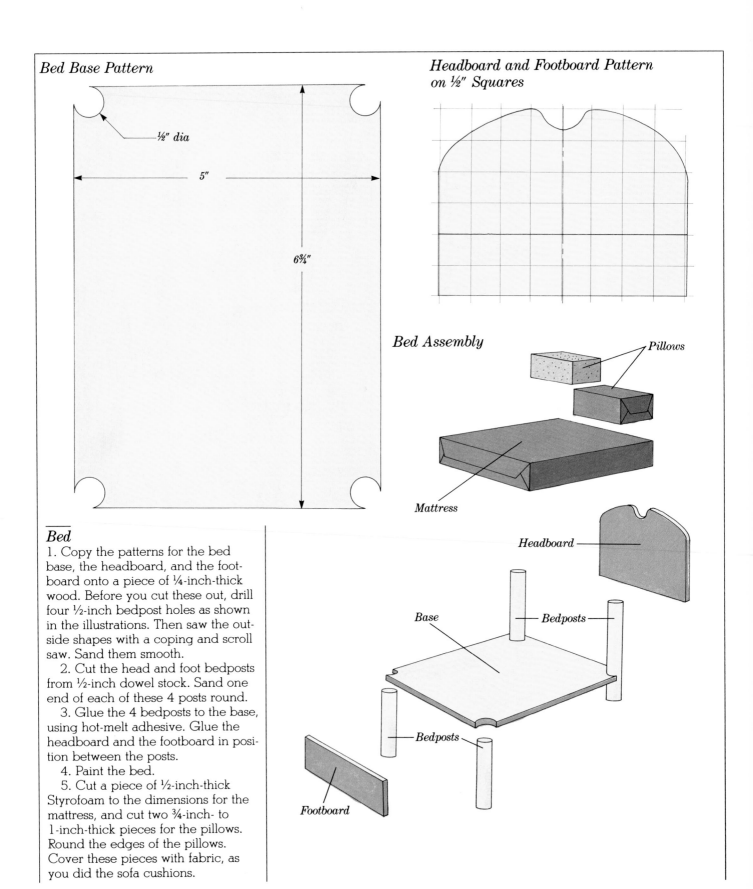

½" dia

5"

6¾"

Headboard and Footboard Pattern
on ½" Squares

Bed Assembly

Pillows

Mattress

Headboard

Base

Bedposts

Bedposts

Footboard

Bed

1. Copy the patterns for the bed base, the headboard, and the footboard onto a piece of ¼-inch-thick wood. Before you cut these out, drill four ½-inch bedpost holes as shown in the illustrations. Then saw the outside shapes with a coping and scroll saw. Sand them smooth.

2. Cut the head and foot bedposts from ½-inch dowel stock. Sand one end of each of these 4 posts round.

3. Glue the 4 bedposts to the base, using hot-melt adhesive. Glue the headboard and the footboard in position between the posts.

4. Paint the bed.

5. Cut a piece of ½-inch-thick Styrofoam to the dimensions for the mattress, and cut two ¾-inch- to 1-inch-thick pieces for the pillows. Round the edges of the pillows. Cover these pieces with fabric, as you did the sofa cushions.

Sofa and Easy Chair Pattern on ½" Squares

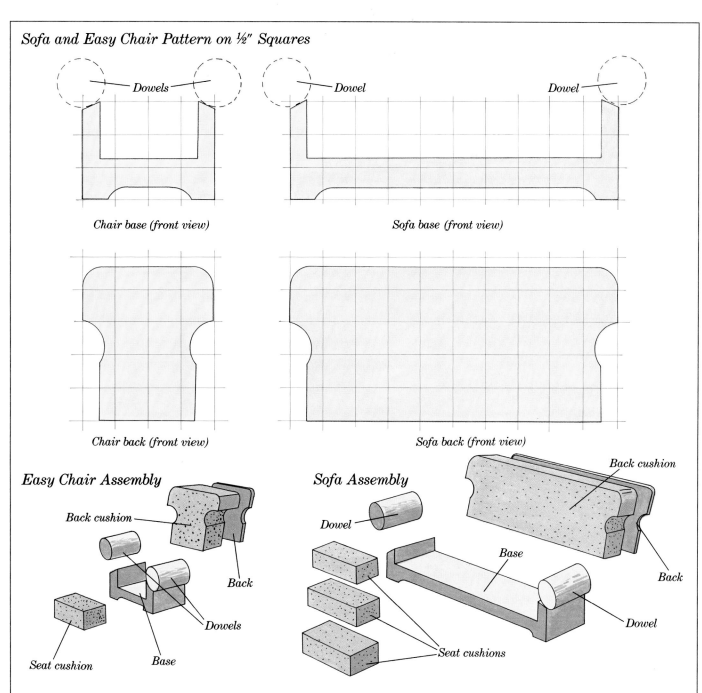

Chair base (front view)

Sofa base (front view)

Chair back (front view)

Sofa back (front view)

Easy Chair Assembly

Back cushion

Back

Dowels

Seat cushion

Base

Sofa Assembly

Back cushion

Dowel

Base

Back

Dowel

Seat cushions

Sofa and Easy Chairs

1. Draw the shape of the sofa base and the easy chair bases on a piece of 1½-inch-thick 2 by 6 material. Use a coping or scroll saw to cut these shapes out. Sand the bases, removing saw marks and rounding the corners.

2. Cut the sofa and easy chair backs from ⅛-inch stock. Sand these smooth.

3. Saw the 6 sofa and easy chair arms from pieces of ¾-inch dowel. Round the ends of these arm pieces with sandpaper.

4. Glue the backs to the bases with hot-melt adhesive. Glue arms in place.

5. Cut some ⅝-inch-thick Styrofoam to form the shapes of the sofa and chair seats and back cushions. Round the edges.

6. You can cover cushions with fabric or paint them to match the rest of the piece. To use fabric, cut and glue some scraps of fabric around the Styrofoam cushion pieces. Paint the furniture before attaching the cushions if you've used fabric upholstery.

7. Glue the cushions in place. Paint the furniture, if you haven't done so already.

INDEX

U.S./Metric Measure Conversion Chart

Symbol	When you know:	Multiply by: (Formulas for Exact Measures)	To find:	Rounded Measures for Quick Reference		
Mass (Weight)						
oz	ounces	28.35	grams	1 oz		= 30 g
lb	pounds	0.45	kilograms	4 oz		= 115 g
g	grams	0.035	ounces	8 oz		= 225 g
kg	kilograms	2.2	pounds	16 oz	= 1 lb	= 450 g
				32 oz	= 2 lb	= 900 g
				36 oz	= 2¼ lb	= 1000 g (1 kg)
Volume						
tsp	teaspoons	5.0	milliliters	¼ tsp	= 1/24 oz	= 1 ml
tbsp	tablespoons	15.0	milliliters	½ tsp	= 1/12 oz	= 2 ml
fl oz	fluid ounces	29.57	milliliters	1 tsp	= 1/6 oz	= 5 ml
c	cups	0.24	liters	1 tbsp	= ½ oz	= 15 ml
pt	pints	0.47	liters	1 c	= 8 oz	= 250 ml
qt	quarts	0.95	liters	2 c (1 pt)	= 16 oz	= 500 ml
gal	gallons	3.785	liters	4 c (1 qt)	= 32 oz	= 1 liter
ml	milliliters	0.034	fluid ounces	4 (1 gal)	= 128 oz	= 3¾ liter
Length						
in.	inches	2.54	centimeters	⅜ in.		= 1 cm
ft	feet	30.48	centimeters	1 in.		= 2.5 cm
yd	yards	0.9144	meters	2 in.		= 5 cm
mi	miles	1.609	kilometers	2½ in.		= 6.5 cm
km	kilometers	0.621	miles	12 in. (1 ft)		= 30 cm
m	meters	1.094	yards	1 yd		= 90 cm
cm	centimeters	0.39	inches	100 ft		= 30 m
				1 mi		= 1.6 km
Temperature						
°F	Fahrenheit	5/9 (after subtracting 32)	Celsius	32° F		= 0° C
°C	Celsius	5/9 (then add 32)	Fahrenheit	68° F		= 20° C
				212° F		= 100° C
Area						
in.²	square inches	6.452	square centimeters	1 in.²		= 6.5 cm²
ft²	square feet	929.0	square centimeters	1 ft²		= 930 cm²
yd²	square yards	8361.0	square centimeters	1 yd²		= 8360 cm²
a.	acres	0.4047	hectares	1 a.		= 4050 m²